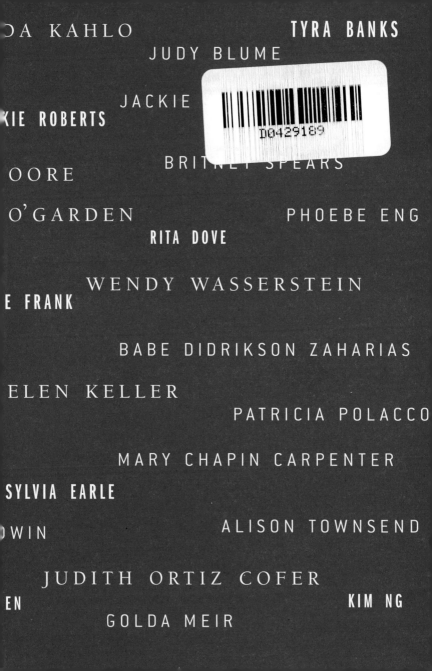

DA KAHLO   TYRA BANKS

JUDY BLUME

JACKIE

KIE ROBERTS

BRITNEY SPEARS

OORE

O'GARDEN   PHOEBE ENG

RITA DOVE

WENDY WASSERSTEIN

E FRANK

BABE DIDRIKSON ZAHARIAS

ELEN KELLER

PATRICIA POLACCO

MARY CHAPIN CARPENTER

SYLVIA EARLE

WIN   ALISON TOWNSEND

JUDITH ORTIZ COFER

EN   KIM NG

GOLDA MEIR

D0429189

THE GREATNESS OF GIRLS

THE GREATNESS OF GIRLS

FAMOUS WOMEN TALK ABOUT GROWING UP

SUSAN STRONG

*To the Greatness of
Julia & Sophia!
with love,
Susan Strong*

**Andrews McMeel
Publishing**

Kansas City

01 02 03 04 05 RDC 10 9 8 7 6 5 4 3 2 1

Library of Congress Cataloging-in-Publication Data

Strong, Susan, Mrs.
   The greatness of girls : famous women talk about growing up / Susan Strong.
      p. cm.
   Includes index.
   ISBN 0-7407-1880-0
   1. Teenage girls. 2. Adolescence. 3. Women—Biography. I. Title.
HQ798 .S825 2001
305.4'092'2—dc21   2001022655

Book design by Lisa Martin

ATTENTION: SCHOOLS AND BUSINESSES

Andrews McMeel books are available at quantity discounts with bulk purchase for educational, business, or sales promotional use. For information, please write to: Special Sales Department, Andrews McMeel Publishing, 4520 Main Street, Kansas City, Missouri 64111.

FOR BOB, OLIVIA, AND CAITLIN

AND IN MEMORY OF MY MOM,
MARY LOUISE WOLD STRONG

CONTENTS

ACKNOWLEDGMENTS

I could not have seen this book through its completion without the love and guidance of so many people. I extend my most earnest thanks to the following angels:

To all the women who opened their hearts on these pages, I thank you for sharing your stories. Your courage to persevere and your desire for others to learn from your experiences is the essence of this book. I was moved and inspired daily as I read and listened to your remarkable tales. Because of you, this book has exceeded my original expectations. You are my heroes, and I am forever grateful for your participation.

Marla Miller, editor, mentor, and most of all friend, gave this book life. Your knowledge of the process (armed with your crafty red pen and infectious laugh) helped me create the book I first imagined. Your unwavering devotion kept me on track. I treasure you and your talents.

A special thank-you to my agent, Alison Picard, for first believing in the book and then finding it the right home at Andrews McMeel. Enormous gratitude to my editor, Jean Lucas. You provided valuable ideas and kind encouragement when this writer needed it most.

To Mary Strong's trophies, my brothers and sisters, Jeff, Sid, Tracy, and Amy. My youth was spared much angst thanks to your constant teasing, love, and support. I am a better person because of each of you. To my parents, Jack and Carol Strong and Kay and Bob Pohl. Your love has no boundaries.

To Lynette Hall, the queen of pop culture and class. To the effervescent Susan Shand who inspires by example. And to nature's friend and mine, Becky Swift. I am honored to have you all at my side.

To the Florida girls, Dana Farley and Susan Murray, high school soul mates and lifelong friends. Here's to surviving our own adolescence. This book is for you.

My real-life teenage audience of nieces and friends provided me with honest opinions and clever ideas to make this a better book. Thanks, Jordan Hall, Hannah Lacko, Tara Pohl, Alivia and Jessica Miller Mazura, Molly Strong, Mandy, Maren, Kristen, and Kathryn Zielony for letting me test the waters on you.

This idea was born in the children's section at my local bookstore, Chaucers. Heartfelt thank-yous to the childrens' book expert Kristine Kelly; Carolyn Gell, who cheered me on; Maryejo del Meijer, who nurtured me through the process; Lee Wardlaw, for giving me hope;

Joy Kunz, who walked by my side; and to my first mentor, Juli Davidson, for putting a pen in my hand.

To the finest friend a woman could have, Charles Champlin. Our relationship was handed to me from heaven. Thank you for listening and helping me grow.

To the greatness of our girls, Olivia and Caitlin Pohl. I wrap my love around your beauty, talent, and dreams. And most of all, my deepest love and gratitude to Bob Pohl, who belongs in the Husbands' Hall of Fame. Your loving affection, endless support, and enthusiastic reactions to every idea (and every new hairdo) make me realize how blessed I am to call you husband and best friend. Every day you set the pace with your passion for life.

INTRODUCTION

❧

Life moves fast these days. Homework dominates, activities fill up any extra time, and family responsibilities often fall by the wayside just because it's hard to stay on top of it all. You are on the receiving end of a lot of mixed messages—from your parents, teachers, classmates, and the media. You look over your shoulder and wonder why other girls look like they have it together. But it's just not so. It only appears that way. Everyone goes through the same stuff. That's why I created *The Greatness of Girls.* It's a book you can pick up again and again and know you are not alone.

Think of *The Greatness of Girls* as your very own support system. The women in this book will inspire and encourage you. Their stories will comfort you, their accomplishments reassure you, their struggles help you feel a bit braver. Sigourney Weaver is a confident actor tackling difficult roles that she masters with aplomb. Yet during drama school she was told that she'd never succeed because she couldn't act. Sigourney had faith in herself and kept going. To her, life is a continuing education, and she welcomes its challenges because she knows it's from failing that we grow. Maya Angelou, one of our country's most admired poets, witnessed adversity firsthand growing up in a time when racial prejudice was openly practiced. She chose to carry on and express herself through her writing, acting, and music, thus giving African-Americans a voice they can call their own. Maybe you can relate. Maybe you can gain some insight by reading about the lives of women who made a difference.

As for me, when I was your age, my life was a roller coaster of emotions. I am the fourth of five children, and the expectation to be "nice" stifled my true voice. My mom and dad almost split up, and that jolted me out of my junior high routine. Fortunately, they stayed together and we started a new life, moving to Florida from my Minnesota roots. Entering the ninth grade in the middle of the school year was so embarrassing. I was the self-conscious new kid in the wrong clothes. It had been an all-boys' school; my class was the first to allow girls. In a sea of mostly boys, I desperately zoomed in on the only two girls in the class. Our eyes met—we became best friends and remain so today.

Hanging out with my new friends was my only concern. Unfortunately, my social life took priority over my studies, and the consequence I paid was failing ninth grade. I thought my life was over. But it wasn't. Repeating ninth grade turned out to be a blessing in some ways. I eventually saw it as a second chance. My old friends didn't care that I was a year behind them, and I even made new ones. I decided to change the direction of my life by goofing off less and listening more. The result? I graduated from high school with honors. After college in Boston I landed a great job at MTV in New York City. My crooked journey led me down a path with wonderful opportunities, because I opened my mind and trusted my instincts.

The women found in the pages of *The Greatness of Girls* are from various eras, backgrounds, and cultures. Their accomplishments in political science, marine biology, sports, and the arts help define who they are professionally. Yet their personal stories all have a common thread. They challenged themselves, embraced the good, overcame the bad, and listened to that often loud (and sometimes muffled) voice inside that said, "You can do it." It is my hope that as you learn about these great women, you will identify with the roads they traveled and in turn realize that many opportunities await you.

You belong with these extraordinary women who have made the world a better place. The only difference is your adventure is just beginning. *The Greatness of*

Girls is a personal guide that will help you travel down the path of growing up. Find some strength and encouragement in these pages. Life is a long, joyful, and bumpy ride. Have faith in yourself and enjoy the Greatness of You.

> With my fondest admiration,
> Susan Strong

FAMILY
CONNECTIONS

❧

Find Harmony at Home

You feel ready. You're growing up. That means taking chances, making meaningful decisions. You can stay out later, stay home alone, and go out with friends on your own. You're ready to prove yourself, show you can handle responsibility. And just as you prepare to make the big leap and attack the next challenge, your mom and dad enter the picture. You hear the familiar comments: "Be home by ten o'clock." "Who are you going with?" "You are not wearing that to school." As much as they want you to succeed, their approach can sometimes differ from yours. These emotional times, mixed with pleasure and pain, offer lessons that, once learned, will empower and encourage you to become the best you can be.

Trying to see your parents' point of view can be a

1

challenge in itself. Take a step back and think about your relationships with everyone in your family. Where would you be without your dad embarrassing you by making silly remarks every time he picks you up from school? A lot happier? Or would life be a little less interesting? When your mom remarried and went back to work, everything changed. Grandma pitches in, but it's not the same. And sure, your siblings annoy you endlessly, but you know, deep down, they would do anything for you. Sometimes it's complicated, but these are memories for a lifetime.

The family experiences of the famous women found in *The Greatness of Girls* all differ. Some had a tough go of it, some felt overprotected, while others were grateful for the love and support they received. Some women named their mothers as best friends; others turned to their dads for love and emotional support. Divorce left its mark on many. All tried to make the best of unfortunate situations. Just like those of the famous women quoted in these pages, our lives are unique stories that make us who we are. Our families are the people who love us no matter what. They are the first ones to recognize our talents, the first to point out our faults, the first to nurture us into caring, responsible adults.

る

The family. We were a strange little band of characters trudging through life sharing diseases and toothpaste, coveting one another's desserts, hiding shampoo, borrowing money, locking each other out of rooms, inflicting pain and kissing to heal it in the same instant, loving, laughing, defending and trying to figure out the common thread that bound us all together.

Erma Bombeck

QUEEN LATIFAH

Musician, actor, author, television talk-show host

born: 1970

WHO SHE IS:

The first female rap artist, whose socially conscious lyrics have won her national attention. Queen Latifah runs her own company, has acted in several television series and movies, and hosts her own daily talk show, *Latifah.* She wrote *Ladies First: Revelations of a Strong Woman,* an empowering story about her journey.

*A*ll women are queens," says the rap artist Queen Latifah, who brightens any room she enters. Born Dana Elaine Owens, at age eight she had a keen desire to redefine who she felt she really was. She chose her new name, Latifah, because of its meaning: delicate, sensitive, and kind. Queen Latifah credits her parents for giving her confidence and her older brother, Winki, for giving her courage. Her life hit a major bump in 1978, when her parents informed them that they were splitting up. Queen Latifah remembers it as a major turning point in her life.

❧

My father, like my mother, also taught me how to be a queen. He gave me his love with hugs and kisses. And he taught me that I could be strong without being a bully. He taught me that it was okay to be a good guy. And he taught me that there was nothing that I couldn't do.

When I was with him, I climbed trees and jumped fences. When I came home all scraped up with cuts and bruises on my knees, arms, and elbows, he didn't try to make me stop. He would tease me instead: "Your legs are too pretty to have those marks on them," he'd say. "We'll just have to get them fixed." I didn't care about those scrapes, because I was having fun. And more than that they told the world that I had been out braving peril. Those "marks" were the marks of a girl unafraid.

My mother had her role. She was the talker, the nurturer. And he had his. He brought out my fearless, aggressive side; he filled in the blanks of my personality. And it was like a harmony. Before they separated, my parents complemented each other when it came to raising us kids. I needed the balance of my mother's strong yet gentle manner that was always encouraging me and my father's no-b.s., always-pushing-for-more attitude. Together my parents laid a solid foundation for both my brother and me. I didn't realize how much I needed both of them until he wasn't there. When we left our father, it was difficult not only for my mother but for me and Winki, too. There was a hole in our lives.

• • • • • •

JANE GOODALL

Primatologist, National Geographic Society explorer in residence

born: 1934

WHO SHE IS:

In 1960 Jane Goodall arrived in Africa's Gombe Forest to study chimpanzees. Her findings have revolutionized our understanding of primate behavior. Her research revealed that chimpanzees have distinct personalities, that they are meat eaters, and that they use blades of grass as tools to pluck termites from a mound. Today the Jane Goodall Institute continues observing chimpanzees, and Dr. Goodall travels over three hundred days a year, speaking to audiences about her studies, preserving the environment, and spreading her primary message—that we must be respectful of all life and that every single person can make a difference.

At age eleven, reading the tales of Tarzan, king of the jungle, was as close as Jane Goodall could get to Africa—that faraway place she dreamed of traveling to even then. She grew up to realize her dream, spending much of her life in the wild in Africa, studying chimpanzees: their habits, personalities, and the intimate, humanlike bond between mother and child. Jane's *mother, Vanne, was her greatest source of inspiration. After Jane's father enlisted in World War II, she, her mother, and her sister moved to her grandmother's house near the English Channel. It was here that her mother saved their lives on what seemed to be an ordinary day at the beach.*

ತಿ

Even we had one narrow escape. It was during the fourth summer of the war. Judy and I, with our best friends Sally and Susie, were spending a week's holiday a few miles along the coast where one could actually get onto the sand (England was prepared for a possible German invasion, so most of the coastline was barricaded by miles and miles of barbed wire). One day, as our mothers sat on the sand and we played at the shore, my mother suddenly decided to take a different route back to our little guest house—a very long way around that meant we would miss lunch but she was determined. Ten minutes after we set off, walking over some sand dunes, we heard the faint sound of a plane flying very high, heading south toward the sea. I can still remember, absolutely vividly, gazing up and seeing two tiny black objects, looking no bigger than cigars at that height, dropping from the plane into the blue, blue sky. German bombers often dumped their bombs along the coast if they had not managed to get rid of them on designated targets. It was safer when they met our planes on their way home. I can still remember our two mothers telling us to lie down, then trying to shield us with their bodies. I can still recall the terrifying explosions as the bombs hit the ground. And one of them made a deep crater halfway up the lane—exactly where we would have been but for Vanne's premonition.

● ● ● ● ● ●

ELEANOR ROOSEVELT
U.S. First Lady, writer, humanitarian
1884–1962

WHO SHE IS:

Known throughout the world for her devotion to human rights, Eleanor Roosevelt was the first wife of a president to take an active role outside the White House. She fought fearlessly for the rights of the poor, women, children, and African-Americans.

Eleanor Roosevelt married her distant cousin Franklin Delano Roosevelt, who later served as president of the United States for over twelve years, until his death in office in 1945. Although shy and preferring the company of family and friends, as the wife of a politician

Eleanor was catapulted into the public eye. She turned a negative into a positive by using her fame to bring attention to how the disenfranchised had to live. Her childhood was not carefree. Her father's alcoholism often caused her parents to separate. Eleanor was lonely and fought frequently with her mother, yet also craved her attention.

ॐ

I slept in my mother's room and remember well the thrill of watching her dress to go out in the evenings. She looked so beautiful, I was grateful to be allowed to touch her dress or her jewels or anything that was part of the vision which I admired inordinately.

My mother suffered from very bad headaches, and I know now that life must have been hard and bitter and a very great strain on her. I would often sit at the head of her bed and stroke her head. People have since told me that I have good hands for rubbing, and perhaps even as a child there was something soothing in my touch, for she was willing to let me sit there for hours on end. As with all children, the feeling that I was useful was perhaps the greatest joy I experienced.

● ● ● ● ● ●

JACKIE
Track and field Olympic and world record champion
JOYNER-KERSEE   born: 1962

WHO SHE IS:

Jackie Joyner-Kersee is an Olympic champion who has become the fastest, and the longest- and highest-jumping female athlete in track and field to date.

Considered by many to be the world's greatest female athlete, Jackie Joyner-Kersee is an inspiration to all, holding the world record in the heptathlon—a track and field competition consisting of seven events. Jackie's determination began at home, when she was growing up in East St. Louis in a less than perfect setting. Jackie was eighteen years old and playing basketball for UCLA when her mother died of meningitis.

❧

My dad, who had been involved in athletics, had a better appreciation of sports than my mom. She didn't quite understand the sports arena, and she was very hesitant at times to allow me to do sports because she thought the best avenue for me was to get an education. She couldn't grasp the idea of her daughter going away for the weekend with strangers, because she didn't know them. My dad explained to her how important this was for me to be able to compete against other girls that were the same age as I was, and to allow me to make new friends from different parts of the country. He always had that vision for me.

My mom was always supportive and eventually began to understand my desire to play, though she always emphasized education first, the reason being she and my dad were just teenagers when they had my older brother. She didn't want me to miss a part of my life and knew firsthand how difficult it was for teenagers to raise kids. She didn't want that happening to her daughter and figured if I stayed focused on education it wouldn't. She really wanted me to make something of my life.

• • • • • •

PHOEBE ENG

Writer, activist

born: 1961

WHO SHE IS:

After practicing law in New York, Hong Kong, and Paris, Phoebe Eng founded *A. Magazine: Inside Asian America,* for the English-speaking, Western-oriented Asian market. She is the author of *Warrior Lessons: An Asian American Woman's Journey into Power* and lectures extensively on empowering women to be true to themselves. An award-winning social activist, Ms. Eng advises many national organizations on race relations. She was a member of the Ms. Foundation delegation to the 1995 UN World Conference on Women in Beijing.

*P*hoebe Eng grew up in New York with her sister and parents, who are first-generation Chinese immigrants. In an environment that minimized her ethnic roots, Phoebe was still heavily influenced by her parents' traditional expectations. Many of her decisions about college and career confused her parents, who didn't always agree with her but understood Phoebe's determination and supported her choices. In Manhattan's Chinatown, Phoebe and her sister often enjoyed a carefree life.

❧

In the dog days of July, when we were overcome with boredom and scorching hot temperatures, my sister and I would fight. Sometimes it was more than our mother could bear, and so she'd banish us to our cousin Shirley's house, a small apartment on Mott Street, deep in Manhattan's Chinatown. It was like being sent to an amusement park. While Chinatown adults slaved long hours in the restaurants and garment factories, we kids did anything we wanted almost all of the time.

In Chinatown, we'd spend long afternoons at the Pagoda Theater, a sticky-floored movie house where we'd watch the best double-feature kung fu films that I can remember. That's where I learned to read as fast as a Model Minority bullet, speeding through the English subtitles that flashed across the screen with a few seconds left to see the pictures. My favorite fighting women in their fine medieval Chinese costumes would somersault from roof to roof, their gossamer layers of white billowing as they brandished weird-looking weapons, sticks and swords and fireballs, against evil forces. They could harness the wind and make worlds collapse. As in all great kung fu movies, they'd shout out their maneuvers so that their opponents would know, moments before their demise, the debilitating blow that would deliver them into oblivion. "*Double Snake Whirlwind!*" she'd scream, and a gale would blow with such force that all her opponents would be sucked into the abyss. "*Ladder Technique!*" she'd say, and she'd fly up onto two ladders, using them as makeshift stilts, to gain fighting advantage. Kung fu warrior queens knew they were hot. They never tried to hide. They never screamed in those high-pitched sissy voices the way women in the American movies did.

Those movies would leave Donna (my sister), Shirley and me crazed and adrenaline-charged and ready to test out those new moves as soon as we got back to Shirley's cramped apartment. We would erect barricades with Shirley's plastic-covered, peacock-embroidered sofa cushions and create hidden rooms by draping sheets over her lower bunk beds so that we could reenact the movie scenes. Nerf balls made great fireballs, and chopsticks did well as improvised daggers. We'd fashion our warrior hair so that it flowed like fountains from the top of our heads. We'd leap from the top bunk bed down to the double bed only inches away, imagining that we were flying around in the small bedroom where Shirley's entire family of five slept. And when Shirley's brother Steven came home from school, we would attack him in cleverly engineered surprise ambushes.

● ● ● ● ● ●

GOLDA MEIR
Israeli political leader
1898–1978

WHO SHE IS:

Golda Meir, an Israeli political leader, dedicated herself to Zionism, a worldwide Jewish movement that resulted in the establishment and development of the state of Israel. Ms. Meir lived on a kibbutz in Palestine, fought for Jewish refugees to be allowed into Palestine, and signed her country's Declaration of Independence when Israel became a state in 1948. She was a member of Israel's parliament for twenty-five years and elected its fourth prime minister in 1969, retiring in 1974.

Until she was eight years old Golda Meir lived in Russia with her Ukrainian-Jewish family. They struggled to make a living and faced anti-Semitism daily. In search of a better life her father moved the family to Milwaukee, Wisconsin, where Golda was encouraged to get an education. She adored school and had dreams of becoming a teacher. However, her parents had other plans for Golda, plans that caused conflict.

❧

When I was fourteen, I finished elementary school. My marks were good, and I was chosen to be class valedictorian. The future seemed very bright and clear to me. Obviously, I would go on to high school and then, perhaps, even become a teacher, which is what I most wanted to be. I thought—and still think today—that teaching is the noblest and the most satisfying profession of all. A good teacher opens up the whole world for children, makes it possible for them to learn to use their minds and in many ways equips them for life. I knew I could teach well, once I was sufficiently educated myself, and I wanted that kind of responsibility. My friends, Regina, Sarah and I talked endlessly about what we would do when we grew up. I remember on those summer evenings how we sat for hours on the steps of my house and discussed our futures. Like teenage girls everywhere, we thought these were the most important decisions we would ever have to make—other than marriage, and that certainly seemed much too remote to be worth our talking about.

My parents, however—as I ought to have understood but did not—had other plans for me. I think my father would have liked me to be educated, and at my Fourth Street graduation ceremony his eyes were moist. He understood, I believe, what was involved; but in a way his own life had defeated him, and he was unable to be of much help to me. My mother, as usual and despite her disastrous relationship with Sheyna, my older sister, knew exactly what I should do. Now that I had finished elementary school, spoke English well and without an accent and had developed into what the neighbors said was a *dervaksene shein meydl* (a fine, upstanding girl), I could work in the shop full time and sooner or later—but better sooner—start thinking seriously about getting married, which, she reminded me, was forbidden to women teachers by state law.

If I insisted on acquiring a profession, she said, I could go to secretarial school and learn to become a shorthand typist. At least, I wouldn't remain an old maid that way. My father nodded his head. "It doesn't pay to be too clever," he warned. "Men don't like smart girls." As Sheyna had done before me, I tried every way I knew to change my parents' mind. In tears, I explained that nowadays an education was important, even for a married woman, and argued that in any case I had no intention whatsoever of getting married for a very long time. Besides, I sobbed, I would rather die than spend my life—or even part of it—hunched over a typewriter in some dingy office.

• • • • • •

FRIDA KAHLO   Painter   1907–1954

WHO SHE IS:

The legendary Mexican artist, Frida Kahlo painted vivid self-portraits. Her topics include depictions of herself suffering as a result from a childhood accident, her turbulent marriage to her fellow artist the muralist Diego Rivera, and her commitment to the Mexican Revolution. As seen in most of her paintings, Ms. Kahlo dressed in colorful

Mexican costumes, elaborately braiding her hair with flowers and ribbons to identify herself with her country's heritage.

Frida Kahlo's father was a German-Jewish photographer, and her mother was of Mexican descent. She was considered a "tomboy" until polio struck her at age six. Burdened with a limp and a thin leg, she was teased mercilessly yet still managed to swim, play soccer, bicycle, and skate. Her father, who suffered from epilepsy, favored Frida most of his six children. Encouraging her curiosity, he would often take her on his outdoor photography adventures. Bound by their illnesses, Frida and her father took care of each other.

かで

Many times when [my father] went walking with his camera on his shoulder and me by the hand, he would suddenly fall. I learned how to help him during his attacks. My childhood was marvelous because though my father was sick, he was able to set such a fine example of a tender man who loved his work [photographer and also painter] and above all, understood my particular problems.

• • • • • •

COKIE
Broadcast journalist, author

ROBERTS
born: 1943

WHO SHE IS:

Cokie Roberts is chief congressional analyst covering politics, Congress, and public policy for both ABC News and her weekly television show, *This Week with Sam Donaldson and Cokie Roberts.* She is also a news analyst for National Public Radio and author of *We Are Our Mothers' Daughters,* a book highlighted by personal anecdotes that addresses significant issues facing women today.

Cokie Roberts came home from the hospital Mary Martha Corinne Morrison Claiborne Boggs. Her brother dubbed her Cokie. The name stuck. Her father was a U.S. congressman, which meant Cokie grew up spending half the year in Louisiana and the other half in Washington, D.C. Cokie's mother juggled many tasks, but her number-one priority was always her family. She inspired Cokie, infusing her with the gifts of confidence and humor.

❧

Mamma could always be counted on to come through. Intellectually, I know that she was actually away a lot of the time when we were growing up. She was off campaigning for Daddy, or accompanying him on some official trip. She always worked—for him, for the party, for the community. Even so, as I resurrect those childhood pictures in my memory, they all include Mamma. To me, she was the most beautiful woman on earth, and she seemed a constant presence. When I was little I used to fake being sick so I could stay home and play with her. She knew what I was doing, but never let on. Now I realize how many cancellations and rearrangements must have followed in the wake of my announcements that I didn't feel quite up to going to school that day. Some of the time, she'd check in on me and go about her work, leaving me with Emma Cyprian, the housekeeper, who was a much sterner taskmaster. On the rare occasions when I was really sick, Mamma would do something special, like make doll clothes with me, or whip up a bowl of my favorite dessert, floating island, a custard with islands of meringue floating on top. . . .

Barbara [Cokie's sister], who had appointed herself my teacher, became completely exasperated with me when I was about six years old because she couldn't teach me how to tell time. I remember Mamma making a clock out of a paper plate with construction paper hands. We sat at the edge of her bed, going over it again and again. I never caught on. Finally she just burst out laughing, and it was all okay. I'm sure I remember the episode so well because I was convinced I was a dumbbell, a view my sister was always ready to endorse, until Mamma's laugh just made it all seem silly. That's what she's always done, instill confidence, usually by some action—a hug, a call, a laugh, rather than words. When I was older and various activities kept me at school long after the buses and car pools had departed, it was always my mother who would uncomplainingly fetch me and my friends, and take them all home or back to our house for the night, thereby silently endorsing our endeavors. It was our house where people and parties were welcome.

● ● ● ● ● ●

BEVERLY CLEARY

Children's author

born: 1916

WHO SHE IS:

Beverly Cleary has written over thirty-five award-winning books about real-life kid adventures. Her memorable creations include the title characters in *Ramona the Pest, Henry Huggins,* and *The Mouse and the Motorcycle.* Ms. Cleary has sold over ten million copies of her books and receives more than one hundred fan letters a day.

Growing up during the Depression was tough for Beverly Cleary. Food was scarce and her father was often without work. Beverly had a very tense relationship with her controlling mother. Because she was an only child, every move Beverly made was critically judged. She often escaped to the home of her best friend, a place she felt she could be herself. Upon returning from vacation with her friend and feeling content with her tanned skin, Beverly finally responded to her mother's disapproving welcome.

❦

Sunday evening, when Mr. Klum left me at the foot of our driveway, I felt serene, sun-tinged, and happy. Mother's first words were "Beverly! You've ruined your complexion!" I flopped into the nearest chair. "Mother," I said, pleading and without anger, "it does seem as if no matter what I do, you make me feel guilty."

"Why, that's ridiculous," she said.

Somehow I found the courage to contradict. "No, it isn't ridiculous. You do make me feel guilty," I insisted, still without anger. I wanted so much to talk honestly with Mother, to tell her my feelings, to become her friend.

Mother stiffened, her mouth a straight line. "Well, excuse me for living," she said.

For the first time, I understood that I was afraid of Mother for the guilt she made me bear, and that I could never have an honest conversation with her. The woman I wanted for a friend would always be right; I would always be wrong. I have never understood why, for Mother was genuinely kind to others and could be kind to me when I did exactly as she wished.

• • • • • •

DORIS KEARNS GOODWIN

Writer, biographer, political commentator

born: 1943

WHO SHE IS:

Doris Kearns Goodwin worked with President Lyndon Johnson and assisted him with his memoirs. She is the author of four books, *The Fitzgeralds and the Kennedys, Lyndon Johnson and the American Dream,* the Pulitzer Prize winner *No Ordinary Time: Franklin and Eleanor Roosevelt: The Home Front in World War II,* and her memoir, *Wait Till Next Year.* Ms. Goodwin is a regular contributor to PBS's *The NewsHour with Jim Lehrer,* and she is also an expert on baseball.

At age six, when she was given her first baseball scorecard, Doris Kearns Goodwin and her father bonded forever. It was the 1950s, when A-bomb drills were conducted in schools as regularly as fire drills are today and the fear of catching polio permeated everyone's mind.

Doris found comfort at home wrapped in the support of her parents and two sisters. Her father suffered as a child, yet he never dwelled on his youth, only encouraged his daughters to speak their minds and stand up for their beliefs. His greatest gift was recognizing that his girls deserved the same dreams and rights as boys.

৫৩

My father never accepted the cultural conventions that crushed the ambition and imagination of so many girls. He did not agree that girls should subdue their competitive instincts, or alter their behavior to make themselves attractive to men. He urged me to run for class office, try out for the school plays, and speak up in class if I had something to contribute. When he learned I was going to see a cowboy movie I had already seen and disliked just to please a boy, he shook his head disapprovingly. "You wasted your time once," he said. "Don't do it twice." Elaine's [Doris's friend] feelings that her parents had invested their energy in promoting her brother Gary's aspirations while counseling her to conceal her own gifts and desires was shared by many young girls whose brothers became the focus of their parents' ambitions. Perhaps my father's attitude was different because he had no sons, or perhaps it could be traced to his love for his sister, Marguerite, who had been his closest childhood companion.

● ● ● ● ● ●

Olympic Gold Medalist, forward
for the Women's National Basketball
Association Houston Comets

SHERYL SWOOPES

born: 1971

WHO SHE IS:

Sheryl Swoopes, an Olympic Gold Medalist, is the leading scorer for the WNBA Houston Comets and often voted Most Valuable Player. The Comets have won three WNBA championships under her leadership. Sheryl is also the first female athlete to have a Nike basketball shoe—Air Swoopes—named after her.

Sheryl Swoopes hated being called Legs in elementary school, but now, at six feet, she loves what her long legs enable her to do on the basketball court. As a kid she couldn't wait to get home from school and play with her two brothers. But Mom was there: "Study first, basketball later." Sheryl obliged and is grateful for the good grades she earned. In turn, although Sheryl was one of only a few girls interested in the game, her skeptical mom eventually encouraged her passion.

❧

At first, my mom and my brothers thought it was too masculine for me to play basketball. I liked it and I knew I was good at it. Once I got into high school, my performance was proof of my talent. We started to win. My mother was so proud of me and always said how glad she was that I didn't give up. To hear something like that from your brothers and from other people is special, but to hear it from your mom is fantastic. My mom was and is my biggest fan—my number-one supporter. When I was in high school she traveled everywhere and never missed a game. Other than my mom, I didn't have female role models. I didn't have that special someone to look up to and say, "Great, when I get older I want to be like her." I'm proud to be a role model today. If girls want to play basketball, they know that they now have that opportunity to go on and play professionally. I was taught by my mom to do my best, and I am grateful for everything she does for me.

• • • • • •

MARGARET BOURKE-WHITE

Photographer, photojournalist

1904–1971

WHO SHE IS:

Margaret Bourke-White was one of this country's first photojournalists. With a career that spanned over twenty-five years, Ms. Bourke-White earned many "firsts": she was the first photographer for *Fortune* magazine, the first Western photographer allowed in the Soviet Union, the first female photographer for *Life* magazine, and the first female war correspondent, entering combat zones during World War II. She also documented the concentration camps and was well known for her photographs of the Great Depression.

Margaret Bourke-White's mother fostered Margaret's courage by creating games that taught her not be afraid of the dark and to enjoy being alone. Her interest in photography was encouraged by her father, an engineer who introduced her to images of the machine age, such as industrial plants and architecture. When Margaret was a freshman in college, her father died. Needing to work her way through school, Margaret became a photographer. She supported herself by taking photos of campus life and selling them to students.

❧

My father was an abnormally silent man. He was so absorbed in his own engineering work that he seldom talked to us children at all unless we were outdoors, then he became very communicative. During my childhood, we lived in a small New Jersey town, Bound Brook. Nearby, were lovely woods and the low hilly ranges dignified by the name of the Watchung Mountains. I treasured the nature walks Father and I took together. Father could hide in the bushes and whistle bird calls so convincingly that the birds would come to him. He taught me the names of the stars, and how to distinguish the harmless snakes and pick them up without fear.

I realize now how his entire purpose was focused toward attaining this self-set standard, how deep in him the philosophy was: never leave the job until you have done it to suit yourself and better than anyone else requires you to do it. Perhaps this unspoken creed was the most valuable inheritance a child could receive from her father. That, and the love of truth, which is requisite No. 1 for a photographer. In this training, Mother shared. When I was a very small child, if I broke a soup plate, Mother would say, "Margaret, was it an accident or was it carelessness?" If I said it was carelessness, I was punished but if an accident, I was forgiven. I am proud of Mother's vision in knowing how important it is to learn to be judge of one's own behavior. She did well to see that a habit of truth throughout life is more important than the broken soup plates.

• • • • • •

PATRICIA POLACCO

Children's author

born: 1944

WHO SHE IS:

Patricia Polacco writes and illustrates books for children. She has published over twenty-five books, with many stories based on her own childhood experiences. Her titles include *The Keeping Quilt, Pink and Say, Chicken Sunday,* and *Rechenka's Eggs.*

Growing up, Patricia Polacco was surrounded by relatives and friends from Jewish, Russian, African-American, and Irish heritages. From them she learned the art of storytelling. Their stories provided the inspiration for the stories she would later eloquently write and illustrate. Patricia has always loved the power of the written word to evoke emotion, but writing didn't come easily to her. She had a severe learning disability and could not read until she was fourteen years old. She credits her parents, who lived in separate homes, for providing the love and encouragement she needed.

❧

My mother was my very good friend and very influential in my life. She was also a teacher, actress, and heroic, bigger-than-life, funny, absolutely gorgeous person.

Her greatest gift to my brother and me was the gift of confidence. She taught us to always believe in ourselves. Ultimately that love from both her and my father is why I am here, why I didn't commit suicide at age fourteen. She believed in every harebrained scheme we came up with, no matter how frivolous. She never negated our ideas. Sometimes, she'd offer alternatives and say, "I think you can make it." Hearing those words from someone you respect so much is all you need to get you through the toughest times.

My parents divorced when I was three, and my mom took a teaching job in Oakland, California, so I literally split my time between two places. I spent the summers in Michigan with my dad and the winters with my mother. It all worked out wonderfully because they were very good parents and never pitted the children against the other parent. We felt more loved than many kids did whose parents lived in the same home. Still, having divorced parents was tough at times. I remember distinctly, as a tiny little girl, when one of them would come to pick me up, my heart would be breaking for the one I had to leave. I didn't dare cry for fear that the one picking me up would think I didn't want to go. What I learned from this was how to protect others' feelings, sometimes at the expense of my own. I don't think it's possible to come away unscathed from divorce.

A wonderful benefit of the divorce was that both my parents moved back into their parents' homes, so I had the advantage of living with my parents and grandparents. My mother was Jewish and Ukrainian. My dad was Irish and probably baptized Catholic, though I only knew him as a born-again Christian. In fact, I think his religious conversion was at the core of their divorce. He converted and became a zealot after they were married. Before this transition, he had stopped practicing any religion, but then my brother almost died of spinal meningitis. I think my dad saw it as punishment, so he promised God that if my brother lived, he'd return to his faith. My brother survived and my father kept his promise, which just didn't fit with his marriage. His particular sect was Amish-like, complete with dress codes that forbade the women to wear nail polish or lipstick. For a woman like my mother, whose life centered on drama, these restrictions were too confining, so they went their separate ways. Neither parent ever remarried. I think they loved each other more than life itself. They just couldn't be married.

● ● ● ● ● ●

ELLEN GOODMAN

Newspaper columnist, author

born: 1941

WHO SHE IS:

Ellen Goodman adds her personal insight to her biweekly newspaper column about current events, which is nationally syndicated in over four hundred newspapers. Ms. Goodman is also associate editor of the *Boston Globe* and won a Pulitzer Prize for distinguished commentary in 1980.

*E*llen Goodman describes her childhood as happy. She grew up in Brookline, Massachusetts, with her stay-at-home mom and her politician dad. During the school year she participated in school musicals, and she loved playing tennis at summer camp. Although they were more lenient with her than with her older sister, Ellen's parents still expected her to do well in everything she attempted. Pressure? Sure, but she knew it was okay to fail sometimes. "Take chances, follow your instincts, and don't forget your sense of humor" was the advice given by her dad, a funny man who lived his life following this advice.

ও

We were a very close family. Both my parents encouraged me. My dad ran for Congress and was quite well known in the community. People think of running for office as very stressful on the family, but it wasn't for us. We were probably among the very few kids who saw our father's work in a peculiar way. We loved his speeches and enjoyed his successes. We watched him suffer through losses, saw him fail, saw him pick himself up again, put on his tie, and go to work the next day. His work ethic made a very positive impression on me. This was in the 1950s, during the McCarthy era. My dad was a Jewish Democrat running in a Republican non-Jewish area. We visited places middle-class kids didn't usually visit. We would sit at the polls with him all day. I remember this one day, a man came up to me and said he wouldn't vote for my father if he was the last person on earth. I was only thirteen. I wanted to kill him! That experience opened my eyes and thickened my skin.

As for my mother, I once described her as the kind of person who could listen to your problems until even you were bored by them. She was a classic "stay-at-home" mom who was determined to have a peaceful home because her own home hadn't been. She modeled herself after her best friend's mother. She was always home with cookies and milk for us but at the same time never expected or assumed that would be my future. My parents had great expectations of us but were also very loving. The political atmosphere in my house, the vocal expression of opinions, which sometimes turned into arguments, was normal fare. I always had to defend my point of view. I couldn't just say that's the way I felt.

I was the second child. My older sister got a much heavier dose of discipline and was encouraged to set a good example. One of my favorite memories of childhood was when my sister was in the seventh grade and was required to memorize "The Midnight Ride of Paul Revere." My father, in a benign but instructive way, went over it with her for weeks and weeks. Finally one night at the dining room table, I stood up and recited "The Midnight Ride of Paul Revere." Often second children add a lighter touch in the home. Because I wasn't doing things for the first time like my sister was, I had an easier time.

● ● ● ● ● ●

GLORIA STEINEM
Activist, writer, journalist
born: 1934

WHO SHE IS:

The writer and journalist Gloria Steinem has been at the forefront of the women's movement for over thirty-five years. She helped start two magazines, *New York* and *Ms.* magazine, where she is coeditor. She has also spoken on behalf of civil rights, gay rights, and the peace movement. Ms. Steinem's best-selling books are *Outrageous Acts and Everyday Rebellions* and *Revolution from Within*.

*G*loria Steinem opened doors for women when women needed a powerful voice. Fast-forward a few generations, and she is still at the helm, offering a helping hand to women's issues and organizations. When Gloria was a child her mother suffered from severe anxiety and depression and leaned on Gloria to be the family caregiver. From age ten to seventeen Gloria lived with her mother in the upstairs of a deteriorating house that had thin walls and a rarely functioning furnace. During these times Gloria would pretend to be sick with a cold, hoping her mother would magically turn into a cheerful mom who cooked her chicken soup. The attempts failed and only made her mother feel more guilty about not being able to care for her daughter properly. Gloria struggled and tried to make the best of a sometimes grim situation.

૭ৎ

In that house, I remember:
· lying in bed with my mother trying to keep warm while we listened to the live broadcast on the radio of the royal wedding of Princess Elizabeth and Prince Philip and tried to ignore the unmistakable

sounds of the factory worker downstairs beating up his pregnant wife;

- hanging paper drapes I had bought in the dime store;

- stacking books and papers in the shape of two arm-chairs and covering them with blankets;

- evolving my own dishwashing system (I waited until all the dishes were dirty, then put them in the bath-tub); and listening to my mother's high praise for these housekeeping efforts to bring order from chaos, though in retrospect I think they probably depressed her further;

- coming back from one of the Eagles' Club shows where I and other veterans of a local tap-dancing school made ten dollars a night for two shows, and finding my mother waiting with a flashlight and no coat in the dark cold of the bus stop, worried about my safety walking home;

- in good periods when my mother's native adventur-ousness came through, answering a classified ad together for an amateur acting troupe that per-formed Biblical dramas in churches, and doing sev-eral very corny performances of Noah's Ark while my proud mother shook metal sheets backstage to make thunder;

- on a hot summer night, being bitten by one of the

rats that shared our house and its back alley. It was a terrifying night that turned into a touching one when my mother, summoning courage from some unknown reservoir of love, became a calm, comforting parent who took me to a hospital emergency room despite her terror at leaving home.

● ● ● ● ● ●

JUDY BLUME Writer
born: 1938

WHO SHE IS:

Judy Blume is the author of over twenty meaningful and funny books about the struggles and surprises of adolescent life. Titles such as *Are You There God? It's Me, Margaret; Superfudge; Blubber; Just as Long as We're Together;* and *Forever* have won her more than ninety awards. Ms. Blume's readers send her over a thousand letters a month, sharing their feelings and concerns. She has also written three novels for adults.

Her readers consider Judy Blume the master when it comes to knowing what goes on in the head of a young person. A keen memory and ability to access her inner child help her speak the language her readers understand. Judy started out as a shy, small, and skinny kid but gained confidence as she grew older. Her doting and supportive father was a major influence, yet she never felt at ease sharing her true feelings with either of her parents for fear she would disappoint them. Staying true to herself while living up to others' expectations was a struggle for Judy Blume.

೨೦

My father was my fun parent and really very much my nurturing parent. When I was young, he was the one who cut my fingernails, took my temperature when I was sick, and was there for me emotionally and physically. He introduced me to music and philosophy, and encouraged me to "go for it." I enjoyed performing, and often after dinner my father and I would sing and dance together. This was after my brother went to college. My brother was four years older than I, five years ahead of me at school. He left for college when I was starting eighth grade. He was very different from me, in both personality and interests. We weren't close. I never knew what to expect from him. Our mother was shy, quiet, and anxious. She kept everything inside. She never talked to me about anything important, but she let me know in her own way what she expected of me. I was always afraid if she knew the real me, she'd be let down.

● ● ● ● ● ●

KATHARINE GRAHAM

Newspaper executive

1917–2001

WHO SHE IS:

Katharine Graham was chairman of the executive committee and publisher of the *Washington Post,* the family newspaper she took over after her husband's suicide. Considered one of the most powerful women in America, Ms. Graham played a pivotal role in breaking two major news stories: publication of the Pentagon Papers, which revealed the United States' involvement in the Vietnam War, and publication of the Watergate investigation, which became one of the greatest political scandals in American history. At age eighty Ms. Graham won a Pulitzer Prize for her autobiography, *Personal History.*

Known today as the woman behind the Washington Post, *Katharine Graham came from a wealthy family. Unfortunately, she and her four brothers and sisters were often ignored by her parents, whose own lives took precedent over their childrens' daily needs. Consequently, hired help usually tended to the children. Katharine forged her way through shyness and yearned to be more outgoing, like her sisters. Her father was a dominating* *man and successful in the newspaper business (he bought the* Washington Post *in 1933). Whenever she did interact with him, her impulse was always to please him, making her sometimes say and do things against her wishes.*

≈

One of the earliest transactions I had with my father about the future took place when I was about eight. He kept asking if, when I grew up, if I would be his secretary. I had no idea what a secretary was or did, but the whole idea struck me as distasteful. At the time, my father himself seemed to me a rather remote and strange male figure whom I liked from a distance but thought very different. My answer was a constant and firm no. Although I had an awareness that this was a tease, I knew it was something I didn't want to do. However, I had a bank in which you inserted nickels, dimes, and quarters, and when it reached the vast sum of $5.00 it would spring open. I had been collecting coins for months on my tiny allowance, and finally I needed only one nickel to have all this vast wealth at my command. When I asked my father if he would give me a nickel, he said, "Well, now will you be my secretary?" I agreed. I sold out for a nickel. My father would occasionally refer to this in the future, making me slightly puzzled and anxious, but I never thought of reneging on the bargain and was always referred to as his future secretary.

● ● ● ● ● ●

NINA **Broadcast journalist**
TOTENBERG **born: 1944**

WHO SHE IS:

Nina Totenberg is the award-winning legal affairs correspondent for National Public Radio and can be heard regularly on *All Things Considered, Morning Edition,* and *Weekend Edition.* She covers the U.S. Supreme Court, making the legal arguments comprehensible. Ms. Totenberg also writes frequently for major newspapers and magazines.

Nina Totenberg reflects on her summers traveling with her musician father and remembers playing freely all day while he practiced for the evening performances. He encouraged his daughter in many ways. Nina was determined to go into broadcasting at a time when more women were beginning to enter the workforce. Her father gave her that push when she was a child.

☙

Today's girls have many more opportunities available to them than I did. They have role models who have set examples. When I was growing up, we had Nancy Drew, who was just about the only female heroine in popular literature. I used to read biographies about women, when they were available, but girls really had to search for professional role models. Because of this situation, I emulated my father, who always expected so much of me. My father was a concert violinist, and there were some women professionals in his world who would perform standing in front of the orchestra like he did, and he always let me know in some subtle way that I was an equal to them and there was nothing that I couldn't do, as long as I wanted to do it.

• • • • • •

MARGARET MEAD
Anthropologist
1901–1978

WHO SHE IS:

Margaret Mead was an anthropologist known for her groundbreaking understanding of adolescent girls. Her first book, *Coming of Age in Samoa,* studied Samoan adolescent girls in relation to American adolescent girls. Her findings concluded that culture, not genetics, primarily influences personality development.

Margaret Mead's childhood was unconventional compared with those of others growing up in the early 1900s. Margaret moved often with her professor-parents and grandmother, and the experience exposed her to many other ways of life. When she was not in school her grandmother taught Margaret art, music, and classical languages. It was also her grandmother who encouraged Margaret to record daily observations of her sisters and their early developments, an exercise that turned out to be a primer for Margaret's life-long study of anthropology. It was the women in Margaret Mead's early life who first taught her the value of observing others so we might better understand ourselves.

৶৹

I think it was my grandmother who gave me my ease in being a woman. She was unquestionably feminine— small and dainty and pretty and wholly without masculine protest or feminist aggrievement. She had gone to college when this was a very unusual thing for a girl to do, she had a firm grasp of anything she paid attention to, she had married and had a child, and she had a career of her own. All this was true of my mother as well. But my mother was filled with passionate resentment about the condition of women, as perhaps my grandmother might have been had my grandfather lived and had she borne five children and had little opportunity to use her special gifts and training. As it was, the two women I knew best were mothers and had professional training. So I had no reason to doubt that brains were suitable for a woman. And as I had my father's kind of mind—which was also like his mother's—I learned that the mind is not sex-typed.

● ● ● ● ● ●

TYRA BANKS

Fashion model, actress

born: 1973

WHO SHE IS:

Tyra Banks's image has adorned the cover of nearly every major fashion magazine and Victoria's Secret catalog. Ms. Banks founded TZone, a summer camp to encourage independence and high self-esteem among young females. She has also appeared in several movies.

She's a fashion model with a smile that won't quit and the determination to succeed big. Tyra Banks came from a middle-class family and rose to stardom in the modeling business at the young age of sixteen. Although her parents divorced when she was only six, their support and encouragement have given Tyra insight that she shares with other young girls in her beauty book, Tyra's Beauty Inside and Out.

&

The first few years with my new stepdad weren't easy. He was a strict disciplinarian and allowed no room for slacking off. . . . Of course the strict rules caused resentment on my part. . . . I ignored all of his positive personality traits, like the fact that whenever I wanted to talk, he would stop whatever he was doing to listen. Or that he's such a great artist and was willing to share his talents with me, like helping me with my science projects, which were all first-place winners. The more I took the time to get to know my stepfather, the more I realized that we could relate to each other. I found that when I communicated things I was unhappy about directly to him, it created a bond between us. We became comfortable with each other, so comfortable in fact, that we stopped running to my mother all the time to settle disputes. . . . I had to allow myself to meet my stepfather halfway. Just that little step took our relationship forward by leaps and bounds.

Spending more time alone with my mother also helped me to keep strong ties with her. She understood this and made special time just for me or my brother, which showed us she was not being "taken away" by her new husband.

No family is perfect—mine certainly isn't. The key, of course, is to give and take. Through open communication I've never had to doubt my parents' love. It's given me a sense of security in everything I do.

• • • • • •

MARY **Actress** TYLER MOORE born: 1936

WHO SHE IS:

The television and film actress Mary Tyler Moore has been America's favorite TV sweetheart since she was first seen in the 1960s playing the perky newlywed Laura Petrie on *The Dick Van Dyke Show* and then, in the 1970s, the clean-cut, single career woman Mary Richards on *The Mary Tyler Moore Show.* She has appeared in many films, won an Oscar nomination for her role in *Ordinary People,* and was honored with a Special Tony Award for her Broadway performance in *Whose Life Is It Anyway?* Ms. Moore is also the international chairman for the Juvenile Diabetes Foundation. She has lived with diabetes for much of her life.

*S*oon *after Mary Tyler Moore was born her parents moved in with her mother's mother and sister. Mary's mother's drinking and her father's elusive style only*

*added fuel to an already tense situation. For this reason
Grandma and Aunt Bertie became Mary's primary care-
givers. Her childhood revolved around their security and
love, but as she grew older Mary often was distraught
over her living circumstances and worried constantly
about what others thought of her.*

彡

Because of my mother's inability to stop her heavy
drinking, I lived at home only about half the time during my school years. I find it interesting that I have just
now referred to my parents' house as "home." Certainly, it was more comfortable being secure, and out-
wardly loved, with Grandma and Bertie. Yet no matter
how they reassured me that my friends didn't suspect
some mysterious problem with my parents, I remained
self-conscious and guilty about my address.

It was all very embarrassing to me. When I was living with Bertie, why wasn't I living with my parents?
When I was living at home, why was the house so
unkempt, so tiny; why was my mother so often drunk?

The size of the house my parents bought was a
reflection of their tight money situation, but I wondered
at the time if they had counted on my not living there.
It had two bedrooms and one bath. How were they plan-
ning to accommodate the needs of an adolescent girl
and a toddling boy in the same room? As John grew

older, modesty drove me to the living-room couch, where I slept in fear of being spied upon from the outside. The front door was made of panes of glass and was only three feet from my makeshift bed. I feared classmates peering in and seeing me asleep with my mouth open, drooling. I was afraid that one of my friends from school would appear on the front porch and discover that not only did I sometimes live elsewhere, I didn't even have a bedroom at home.

This stuff was very important to me. Everywhere I looked other families seemed normal. They didn't have a lot of money, but their mothers were reliable, their fathers smiled at them, and only sisters shared a room. Looking back on it, I am sure there were some real horror stories I never knew about, but at the time I felt that there was a lot I had to hide.

● ● ● ● ● ●

ANNE FRANK
Writer, Holocaust victim
1929–1945

WHO SHE IS:

Anne Frank became famous after the publication of her remarkable journal, *The Diary of Anne Frank.* The book chronicles the dreams and frustrations of this young girl hiding from the German Nazis.

*T*hrough Anne Frank's diary we learned what life was like inside an Amsterdam attic where this thirteen-year-old, her family, and four others hid from the Nazis during World War II. In spite of the fact that they lived in daily fear for their lives, Anne's diary tells us she experienced the same problems and dreams as other teenage girls. Often she found herself in disagreement with her mother, angry with her sister, Margot, and desperately in need of her father's love and attention. Like many teenage girls, Anne found solace writing in her journal.

❧

It's different with Father. When I see him being partial to Margot, approving Margot's every action, praising her, hugging her, I feel a gnawing ache inside, because I'm crazy about him. I model myself after Father, and there's no one in the world I love more. He doesn't realize he treats Margot differently than he does me: Margot just happens to be the smartest, kindest, the prettiest and the best. But I have a right to be taken seriously, too. I long for something from Father that he's incapable of giving. I'm not jealous of Margot; I never have been. It's just that I'd like to feel that Father really loves me, not because I'm his child, but because I'm me, Anne.

I cling to Father because my contempt of Mother is growing daily and it's only through him that I'm able to retain the last ounce of family feeling I have left. He doesn't understand that I sometimes need to vent my feelings for Mother. I'm the opposite of Mother so of course we clash. I don't mean to judge her, I don't have that right. I'm simply looking at her as a mother. She's not a mother to me—I have to mother myself. I tell myself time and again to overlook Mother's bad example. I only want to see her good points, and to look inside myself for what's lacking in her. But it doesn't work, and the worst part is that Father and Mother don't realize their own inadequacies and how much I blame them for letting me down. Are there any parents who can make their children completely happy? Sometimes I think God is trying to test me, both now and in the future. I'll have to become a good person on my own, without anyone to serve as a model or advise me, but it'll make me stronger in the end.

● ● ● ● ● ●

KIM NG

Professional baseball executive

born: 1968

WHO SHE IS:

Kim Ng is vice president and assistant general manager of the New York Yankees. As one of only a few high-ranking females in professional baseball,

Ms. Ng oversees day-to-day operations and negotiates contracts for the players. She previously
worked for the Chicago White Sox, where she
began as an intern after graduating from the University of Chicago.

*K*im Ng's family did everything together. They loved
playing tennis, and each weekend the entire family
could be found helping out her grandparents at their
Chinese restaurant on Long Island. Kim had happy memories until age eleven, when her life changed drastically.
Her dad died suddenly in an accident. Until recently Kim
could talk about this trauma only with her husband
because her feelings of loss and guilt were more than
she could bear.

№

There is an event that was earth-shattering for me
and is still extremely difficult to talk about, but with the
possibility that my story may help one person, I have
decided to talk about this very painful part of my life.

When I was eleven years old, my father died in an
accident. At that time, he and my mother were in the
midst of a painful separation, and I blamed him for
much of the reason my family was being torn apart. I
didn't want to talk to him when he called. I didn't want
to see him when he visited. I resented him. I will regret

that until the day I die, because suddenly, without any warning, he was gone from my life. As a kid, I had to deal not only with the death of my father but also with the guilt that maybe he died without knowing that I loved him. I have lived with this guilt for many years.

Now, through watching my mother with my younger sisters and my friends with their children, I realize that parents' love for their child is so strong and resilient, very little can break that bond. Finally, as an adult, I know that my father knew I loved him.

REAL RELATIONSHIPS

❧

Recognize a Helping Hand

Time spent with a good friend is like sinking into a soft, comfy couch that cushions you in love and support. Your better parts come forward—the "true you" emerges. Friends have an amazing effect. They lighten up our serious side, listen to our thoughtful side, and have the knack for showing up just when we need them most.

You may not always keep in touch with the friends you make in school, but you will always remember each one's contribution to your life. The girl you met in gym class, the first one who picked you for her team, the one who always passed you the ball. Or that person you met in the lunchroom on the first day at your new school, the one who offered you pretzels and made you feel less alone. It could be the boy next door who was always there to talk, or your friend's mother who let you cook whatever you wanted in her kitchen, or the teacher who recognized your talents. Our relationships have so many definitions. It's hard to place each one in a specific category, and maybe it's best not to try. Enjoy each relationship for what it offers. Embrace the teachers, the aunts, the neighbors, the friends who appreciate the uniqueness of you.

These famous women share special stories about the people who enhanced their young lives. Without friends and mentors, many might not have become the talented and legendary leaders they are today. Many of these women felt stranded and out of sync with the rest of the world until that one person reached out and, by doing so, set them free. Take a moment to recognize the people who lend you a helping hand. These people often see qualities you don't or can't. No one does life alone. Grab a friend's hand and help each other soar.

ॐ

Oh, the comfort—the inexpressible comfort of feeling safe with a person—having neither to weigh thoughts or measure words, but pouring them all right out, just as they are, chaff and grain together; certain that a faithful hand will take and sift them, keep what is worth keeping, and then with the breath of kindness blow the rest away.

Dinah Maria Mulock Craik

MAYA ANGELOU

Writer, poet, actress, producer, director

born: 1928

WHO SHE IS:

Maya Angelou was asked by President Clinton to read her poem "On the Pulse of Morning" at his inauguration in 1993. Among her many published books, her autobiography *I Know Why the Caged Bird Sings* may be the most recognized and is studied in classrooms around the world.

Born Marguerite Annie Johnson, Maya Angelou suffered an early trauma that changed her life. When she was eight her mother's boyfriend raped Maya. After his trial the man was found beaten to death. Confused, shocked, and devastated by the experience, Maya refused to speak for nearly six years, thinking that if she did others would also die. She and her brother were sent to live in Stamps, Arkansas, with their grandmother, whom Maya called Momma. It was here that Maya's angel, Bertha Flowers, found the life inside Maya's tortured soul. Maya preferred the world of silence, choosing to read rather than speak; Ms. Flowers picked up on this passion and encouraged Maya to speak the words as well as read them.

People, except Momma and Uncle Willey, accepted my unwillingness to talk as a natural outgrowth of a reluctant return to the South. For nearly a year, I sopped around the house, the Store, the school, and the church, like an old biscuit, dirty and inedible. Then I met, or rather got to know, the lady who threw me my first lifeline.

Her skin was a rich black that would have peeled like a plum if snagged, but then no one would have thought of getting close enough to Mrs. Flowers to ruffle her dress, let alone snag her skin. She didn't encourage familiarity. One summer afternoon, sweet-milk fresh in my memory, she stopped at the Store to buy provisions. Another Negro woman of her health and age would have been expected to carry the paper sacks home in one hand, but Momma said, "Sister Flowers, I'll send Bailey up to your house with these things."

She smiled a slow dragging smile, "Thank you, Mrs. Henderson. I'd prefer Marguerite, though." My name was beautiful when she said it. "I've been meaning to talk to her anyway." They gave each other age-group looks.

There was a little path beside the rocky road, and Mrs. Flowers walked in front swinging her arms and picking her way over the stones. She said, without turning her head to me, "I hear you're doing very good school work, Marguerite, but that's all written. The teachers report that they have trouble getting you to talk in class." We passed the triangular farm on our left and the path widened to allow us to walk together. I hung back in the separate unasked and unanswerable questions.

"No one is going to make you talk—possibly no one can. But bear in mind, language is man's way of communicating with his fellow man and it is language alone which separates him from the lower animals." That was a totally new idea to me, and I would need time to think about it.

"Your grandmother says you read a lot. Every chance you get. That's good, but not good enough. Words mean more than what is set down on paper. It takes the human voice to infuse them with the shades of deeper meaning. . . ."

When I finished the cookies she brushed off the table and brought a thick, small book from the bookcase. I had read *A Tale of Two Cities* and found it up to my standards as a romantic novel. She opened the first page and I heard poetry for the first time in my life.

"It was the best of times and the worst of times . . ." Her voice slid in and curved down through and over the words. She was nearly singing. I wanted to look at the pages. Were they the same that I had read? Or were there notes, music, lined on the pages, as in a hymn book? Her sounds began cascading gently. I knew from listening to a thousand preachers that she was nearing the end of her reading, and I hadn't really heard, heard to understand, a single word.

"How do you like that?"

It occurred to me that she expected a response. The sweet vanilla flavor was still on my tongue and her reading was a wonder in my ear. I had to speak.

I said, "Yes, Ma'am." It was the least I could do, but it was the most also.

"There's one more thing. Take this book of poems and memorize one for me. Next time you pay me a visit, I want you to recite." . . .

I was liked, and what a difference it made. I was respected not as Mrs. Henderson's grandchild or Bailey's sister but for just being Marguerite Johnson.

I have tried often to search behind the sophistication of years for the enchantment I so easily found in those gifts. The essence escapes but its aura remains. Childhood's logic never asks to be proved (all conclusions are absolute). I didn't question why Mrs. Flowers had singled me out for attention, nor did it occur to me that Momma might have asked her to give me a little talking to. All I cared about was that she had made tea cookies for me and read to me from her favorite book. It was enough to prove that she liked me.

● ● ● ● ● ●

PATRICIA POLACCO
Children's author
born: 1944

WHO SHE IS:

Patricia Polacco writes and illustrates books for children. She has published over twenty-five books, with many stories based on her own childhood experiences. Her titles include *The Keeping Quilt, Pink and Say, Chicken Sunday,* and *Rechenka's Eggs.*

Patricia Polacco felt dumb in school and was afraid of the constant teasing until her teacher George Felker discovered her problem. She couldn't read or add numbers. Mr. Felker knew Patricia had talent because of her remarkable drawings. He also knew she needed the right tools to overcome her disabilities. Years later Patricia would thank him by writing a children's book, Thank You, Mr. Falker *(she changed his name slightly), dedicating it to the teacher who brought her out of darkness and into the light.*

❧

My adolescence was absolutely grim. Because I am learning disabled—I have dyslexia, dysnumeria, and dysgraphia—academically I could never quite measure up. I didn't have a clue why I couldn't, and that left terrible scars. I thought there was something really wrong with me. I didn't read until I was fourteen and wouldn't have learned then had I not been blessed to have George Felker as my teacher.

Dyslexia is a complicated neurological disorder that causes the brain to jumble words, making it impossible to read. Dysgraphia is part of the disorder that garbles the message being sent from the brain to the hand; therefore writing becomes impossible. I would write in a code I understood but no one else did, which only sealed my doom. Dysnumeria concerns numbers. It wasn't that I didn't understand numbers, the problem was that I couldn't hold a numerical value in my head long enough to work through the simplest problem. So imagine how I felt in school.

George Felker hired a woman, Miss Plessy, to teach me how to read three or four nights a week after school. When I look at any written copy, I look at the negative space around each word, I don't look at the word. I can now do it in lightning speed. It's this message I give learning disabled kids. They think they are dumb, but my experience says most learning disabled individuals are actually quite gifted. I caught up with my classmates big time, so much so that I was taking college English classes while still in high school. But the years of not learning, the years of other kids making fun of me, took a toll. I became the class clown because by being funny I could decide when they laughed at me. That's what got me interested in acting and comedy.

● ● ● ● ● ●

MARY Singer-songwriter
CHAPIN CARPENTER born: 1958

WHO SHE IS:

The guitarist and singer Mary Chapin Carpenter has a crossover appeal that reaches a universal audience. Her songs, a combination of rock, blues, country, and folk, capture the struggles and dreams of day-to-day life. Among her awards are five Grammys, two best female vocalist awards from the Country Music Association, and best female vocalist from the Academy of Country Music.

Mary Chapin Carpenter walked a rocky road through adolescence. Her parents' divorce was quite upsetting; fitting in with peers always a problem. In the midst of this tumultuous time, Mary met Paul, a kind man who she likes to say "dropped from the sky." He offered hope and guidance, suggesting to her that life wasn't as bad as it seemed. They bonded through the power of music

*and his unconditional support of Mary's dreams. Soon
she discovered a happier life.*

ৡৄ

I was around fifteen when my class took a wilderness course in Northern New Jersey called Project Use;
the organization still thrives. Our class went into the
woods, where we learned how to survive in the outdoors.
The school offered this course early in the year, encouraging classmates to bond.

I remember this very well because what came after
was terribly important to me. Tenth grade was such a
difficult age for me. I had every insecurity in the book
and felt impossibly shy and isolated. My parents were
headed for a divorce, and it was pretty tough. We went
on this wilderness course, and I discovered that I loved
being there. I loved being outdoors, and it was during a
difficult procedure that I made friends with my instructor. I was rock climbing, and I was in a rock formation
called a chimney. My back was pushed up against one
slab and my feet were pushed up against another and
I literally had to scooch up and I got stuck. I was scared,
and I started cussing. My instructor, Paul, asked who
was cussing, and I said, "Me! God damn it!" I was a fifteen year-old gutter-mouthed kid. He immediately
started singing a Bob Dylan song a cappella to me. He
just sang this song, and all of a sudden I transcended

my difficulties while stuck between two rocks. Paul became this catalyst in my life, giving me courage and confidence while inspiring me to play more music. Through him I met other great people who are still my friends today. Paul inspired kids and gave them so much. He filled my tank. I looked up to him as a brother, as a father, I loved him as a boy, I loved every part of him. I could rely on Paul as a best friend.

We lost touch for many years, but he was always present in my psyche. Then about eight years ago we hooked up when I was playing a concert in Portland, Oregon. We've been in touch ever since. I always wonder if I would be playing music today if I hadn't met Paul. He had such an amazing influence on my desire to play and sing music.

● ● ● ● ● ●

GOLDA MEIR
Israeli political leader
1898–1978

WHO SHE IS:

Golda Meir, an Israeli political leader, dedicated herself to Zionism, a worldwide Jewish movement that resulted in the establishment and development of the state of Israel. Ms. Meir lived on a kibbutz in Palestine, fought for Jewish refugees to be allowed into Palestine, and signed her country's Declaration of Independence when Israel became a state in 1948. She was a member of Israel's parliament for twenty-five years and elected its fourth prime minister in 1969, retiring in 1974.

Golda Meir's childhood was bittersweet. She liked her new life in America but struggled with her parents' traditional expectations. They wanted her to marry young. In what she thought was the only way to achieve her goals, Golda ran away to her sister Sheyna and brother-in-law Shamai's home. Golda's best friend helped her plan the escape. When she arrived her sister greeted her with open arms and promised to help Golda obtain a good education. Though tormented by her decision, Golda was grateful to have a more promising future.

જ

The last straw was my mother's attempt to find me a husband. She didn't want me to get married at once, of course, but she very much wanted to be sure not only that I would get married at what she considered a reasonable age, but that, unlike Sheyna, I at least would marry somebody substantial. Not rich—that was out of the question—but at least solid. In actual fact, she was already discreetly negotiating with a Mr. Goodstein, a pleasant, friendly, relatively well-to-do man in his early thirties, whom I knew because he used to come into the store now and then to chat for a while. Mr. Goodstein! But he was an old man! Twice my age! I sent a furious letter to poor Sheyna. The reply came from Denver by return mail. "No, you shouldn't stop school. You are too young to work; you have good chances to become something," Shamai wrote. And with perfect generosity: "My advice is that you should get ready and come to us. We are not rich either, but you will have good chances here to study, and we will do all we can for you." At the bottom of his letter, Sheyna wrote her own warming invitation: "You must come to us immediately." There would be enough of everything for all of us, she assured me. All together, we would manage. "First, you'll have all the opportunities to study; second, you'll have plenty to eat; third, you'll have the necessary clothes that a person ought to have.". . .

That letter, written from Denver in November, 1912, was a turning point in my life because it was in Denver that my real education began and that I started to grow up. I suppose that if Sheyna and Shamai had not come to my rescue, I would have gone on fighting with my parents, crying at night and still somehow going to high school. I can't imagine that I would have agreed under any circumstances to stop studying and marry the probably much-maligned Mr. Goodstein; but Sheyna and Shamai's offer was like a lifeline, and I grabbed at it.

When the fateful evening arrived, I sat in the kitchen with my parents as though it were just any ordinary night, but my heart was very heavy. While they drank tea and talked, I scribbled a note for them to read the next day. It was only a few words and not very well-chosen ones at that. "I am going to live with Sheyna so that I can study," I wrote, adding that there was nothing for them to worry about and that I would write from Denver. It must have hurt them terribly to read that note the next morning, and if I were to write it today, I would do so only after much thought and with very great care. But I was under extreme pressure then and only fifteen. Before I went to sleep that night, I went over to Clara's bed and looked at her for a minute. I felt very guilty about leaving her without even saying good-bye, and I wondered what would happen to her now that both Sheyna and I were out of the house, as I thought, for good. Clara was growing up to be the most "American" of us all, a quiet, shy, undemanding little girl, whom everyone liked but to whom I had never paid much attention and whom I didn't really know very well. Now that I was going to leave her, I remember feeling a sudden sense of responsibility. It turned out, though I couldn't have known it then, that being the only child at home would actually make her life easier. My parents were far more lenient with Clara than they had ever been with Sheyna or with me, and mother even spoiled her sometimes. We weren't a demonstrative family, but that night I stroked her face and kissed her, although she slept through my farewell.

● ● ● ● ● ●

DORIS KEARNS GOODWIN
Writer, biographer, political commentator

born: 1943

WHO SHE IS:

Doris Kearns Goodwin worked with President Lyndon Johnson and assisted him with his memoirs. She is the author of four books, *The Fitzgeralds and the Kennedys*, *Lyndon Johnson and the American Dream*, the Pulitzer Prize winner *No Ordinary Time: Franklin and Eleanor Roosevelt: The Home Front in World War II*, and her memoir, *Wait Till Next Year*. Ms. Goodwin is a regular contributor to PBS's *The NewsHour with Jim Lehrer*, and she is also an expert on baseball.

Starting when they were kids, Doris Kearns Goodwin and her best friend, Elaine, shared everything from secrets about boys to their love of baseball. Doris adored Elaine's active household, thriving on the chaos and listening to superstitious folktales told by Elaine's resident grandmother and great-grandmother. When Doris entered junior high her life and Elaine's moved in different directions, yet their common interests kept their friendship strong.

༚

My separation from Elaine, who was one grade behind me and would not enter junior high for another year, made my adjustment more difficult. For as far back as I could remember, Elaine had been my best friend, the first person I called in the morning, the last person I spoke to at night. And even after we finished talking, we continued to send messages across our driveway on our second-story clothesline-pulley. Elaine, full of energy, enthusiasm, and adventure, had planned our days, devised and organized our games, led our expeditions. Her fearless assertion of ideas and opinions commanded my respect. Now, for the first time, we had different schools and different circles of friends.

The distance created by our separate schools was lengthened by the changes of adolescence. The alterations in my body were gradual, and I remained thin and angular. My period came, but without the pain and headaches that Elaine experienced. She was now the tallest person in her class, and her large breasts seemed to encourage boys who had been her friends to jostle her and whisper teasing remarks. Formerly bold and outspoken, Elaine became withdrawn and bookish, slumping forward as she walked and rounding her shoulders protectively. Her confidence, particularly in relation to boys, began to diminish. She even began to worry that her passion for and extensive knowledge of baseball were a liability in a girl and would further alienate the boys. . . .

Ironically, it was the same passion for baseball which Elaine thought alienated boys that provided the surest foundation for our changing friendship. None of my new girlfriends cared about baseball the way we did; none could debate comparative lineups or pitching staffs like Elaine. She was the only one who had seen me jump for joy when the Dodgers won a close game or seen me cry when they lost the playoffs or the World Series. When we talked about baseball, we were simultaneously talking about our shared friendship.

● ● ● ● ● ●

CANDICE BERGEN   Actor

born: 1946

WHO SHE IS:

Candice Bergen is best known for her performance on the award-winning TV sitcom *Murphy Brown,* where she played the title role, an outspoken and opinionated news anchor. She was born into Hollywood aristocracy, daughter of the famous radio host and ventriloquist Edgar Bergen. She began acting in movies in 1965. She is also an accomplished photojournalist and wrote her memoir, *Knock Wood*, in 1984.

Candice Bergen lived a privileged, fast-paced lifestyle in Beverly Hills, where most of her friends were also children of famous parents. Although she tested the waters at her all-girls' high school, she never overstepped the line into real trouble. While she was listening to the latest song on the radio and thinking about boys, her friend Connie taught Candice to be more conscious of social issues outside their school walls.

৯৫

Westlake was not anti-Semitic, at least not in so many words, but in those days you had to look closely to find many Jewish students. A girl named Connie Freiberg had arrived in midterm, and stood out not only as a new girl but also as our class's first Jew. And so her adjustment as a "new girl" was doubly hard. She came from Cincinnati, and her arrival was met with cool curiosity: we virtually ignored her for weeks, then, after a time, began to accuse her of attention-getting behavior. To which she replied, "Of course I'm trying to get attention! No one has talked to me for two months!" That changed abruptly when, in softball in spring semester, she hit a home run. Suddenly everyone wanted her on their team.

The two of us became a team of sorts, a prep school Laurel and Hardy. We had ink fights in study hall, put fetal pigs in each other's lockers, regularly disrupted and got expelled from class. Wavy-haired and wiry-bodied, Connie seemed to go in all directions at once. Her wit was fast and she soon became the court jester of the class. Because she made us laugh, she was sometimes not taken seriously. But she was also the class crusader, and no one taught me more about conscience than Connie: it was from her that I acquired even an incipient political awareness. She was concerned about blacks when all we cared about were boys, and nudged us toward more generous, democratic beliefs, urging tolerance and understanding. I looked to her on any social issue, knowing that hers would be the correct moral position.

● ● ● ● ● ●

ELLEN GOODMAN

Newspaper columnist, author

born: 1941

WHO SHE IS:

Ellen Goodman adds her personal insight to her biweekly newspaper column about current events, which is nationally syndicated in over four hundred newspapers. Ms. Goodman is also associate editor of the *Boston Globe* and won a Pulitzer Prize for distinguished commentary in 1980.

Ellen Goodman walks the talk when it comes to friendship. She considers her friendships among her most treasured assets. It started at home with her first friend, her sister, Jane, then expanded to her cousin Judy, with whom she shared every secret. Ellen took her passion one step further and wrote a book on the importance of friendship (with her best friend, Patricia O'Brien) called I Know Just What You Mean. *According to Ellen and Pat, "Friendship matters a lot to women," and knowing you can count on someone is what real relationships are all about.*

❧

My sister, Jane, and I were very close, even through adolescence. When we were younger, she was kind enough to let me play house with her—just as long as

I would be the sleeping baby. My other closest friend and confidant was my cousin Judy. Judy was the one I talked to about the boys, hair, sex, and clothes. I'm quite tall and blond, and Judy is short and dark. We were a funny pair. We were cousins forming our friendship while sharing the same bunk at summer camp. We didn't live too far apart in Massachusetts, but as kids we thought we did, so the first year or two we wrote to each other constantly, and then we discovered the telephone. We talked all the time. Then Judy moved to my town, Brookline. We spent many nights together, we dated best friends, the whole routine. It was just great to have her nearby.

● ● ● ● ● ●

JUDITH Writer
ORTIZ COFER born: 1952

WHO SHE IS:

Born in Hormigueros, Puerto Rico, Judith Ortiz Cofer is professor of English and creative writing at the University of Georgia and the recipient of numerous awards and grants. Her narrative stories, essays, and poems offer readers insights about growing up Latino. She proudly considers herself an eternal student of the craft and art of poetry.

The urge to tell a story can come at any time for Judith Ortiz Cofer. She was influenced early by her abuela, her grandmother—who could silence a room when she said, "Tengo un cuento,"—I have a story to tell. Her grandfather was a poet. Judith credits him for teaching her the gentleness of words. Blessed with her grandmother's gift for storytelling, Judith could turn an ordinary story into a universal experience. Her uncle, also a storyteller, recognized her talent and was a great support when she needed him most.

❧

I was thirteen. It was the year when I began to feel like Cinderella whose needs were being totally ignored by everyone, including the fairy *madrinas* I fantasized would bring me a new, exciting life with the touch of a magic wand. I had to read all of the virtue-rewarded-by-marriage-to-a-handsome-prince tales at the Paterson Public Library and was ready for something miraculous to happen to me: beautiful clothes, an invitation to a great party, love. Unfortunately there was a dearth of princes in my life. I was not exactly the most popular girl at my school which was filled with Italian and Irish-American princesses. Also, that year I was in the throes of the most severe insecurity crisis of my life. Besides being extremely thin—"skinny bones" was my nickname in the barrio—I was the new girl at the Catholic high school; only one of two Puerto Rican girls attending a small school filled with anglo students. I had also recently been prescribed glasses, thick lenses supported by sturdy black frames. After wearing them for only a few weeks, I developed a semi-permanent ridge on my nose. I tried to make up for my physical deficiency by being well read and witty. This worked fine within my talkative *familia* but not at school among my peers, who did not value eloquence in girls—not more than a well-developed body and social status, anyway.

That Christmas season, the *cuentista* of our family entered my life. My mother's younger brother, Tio, who lived in New York and was the black sheep of the family, returned and brought with him many *cuentos*—stories— about his travels, misadventures, and womanizing— which made him immensely attractive to me. His arrival filled our house with new talk, old stories, and music. Tio liked to tell *cuentos,* and he also like playing his LPs. My mother and he danced to merengues—fresh from the island—which he carried with him as if they were precious crystal wrapped in layers of newspaper. He was the spirit of Navidad in our house, with just a hint of Dionysian about him. Tio enjoyed his Puerto Rican rum, too, so his visits were as short as the festivities, because his bachelor habits eventually wore down my mother's patience.

Tio must have sensed my loneliness that year, for he took it upon himself to spend a lot of time with me the week before Christmas. We went for walks around the gray city, decked out in lights and ornaments like an over-dressed woman, and for pizza downtown. He asked me about my social life and I confessed that my prince had not appeared on our block yet. "Why do you need a prince to have fun?" my uncle asked, laughing at my choice of words. Unlike other adults, he seemed to really listen. Later I understood this was how he learned to tell a story. He told me that I had inherited his and my abuela's gift of the *cuento*. And because he was so unlike my other *carinoso* relatives, who poured the sweet words on us kids without discrimination or restraint (or honesty, I thought), I believed him. I did know how to tell a good story. My mother had warned me that it was Tio's charm, his ability to flatter and to persuade, that usually got him into trouble. Little did she know that I wanted that power for myself, too. The seductiveness and the power of words enticed me.

I remember walking with him past the decorated storefronts of downtown Paterson one evening. My uncle made a game of asking me if I wanted this or that for Christmas. Did I want a Thumbelina doll I had desperately wished for last year? No. I had received a hard plastic doll from one of my grandmothers in Puerto Rico, and my parents had decided that that was enough dolls for me. . . . Did I want jewelry? We looked at all the shiny baubles in the jewelry store window. No. An *azabache* to wear around my neck to ward off the evil eye? No. I laughed. I was too sophisticated then for such superstitious nonsense.

"Surprise me, Tio," I remember saying to him. . . .

On Christmas Eve, the family gathered in our living room. My mother and I had polished the green linoleum floor until it was a mirror reflecting the multicolored lights of the Christmas tree which had done its job of perfuming our apartment with the aroma of evergreen. I was wearing a red party dress my mother had let me choose from her closet and a pair of pumps. I looked at least eighteen, I thought. I put on some of Tio's *pachanga* records on our turntable and waited anxiously for him to come through the door with my gift. What I expected it to be was in the airy realm of a dream. But it would, I knew without a doubt, be magical.

It was late when he finally showed up bearing a brown grocery bag full of gifts, a bleached-blond woman on his arm. After kissing his sisters, waving to me from across the room, and wishing everyone *Felices Pascuas,* he and his partner left for another party. My mother and aunts shook their heads at their brother's latest caprice. My feet hurt in the high-heeled shoes, so I sat out the dances and read one of my mother's books. Some time around midnight I was handed my gifts. Among them there was an unwrapped box of perfume with a card from my uncle. The perfume was Tabu. The card read: *La Cenisosa* from our Island does not get a prince as a reward. She has another gift given to her. I heard a woman tell this *cuento* once. Maybe you can find it in the library or ask Mama to tell it to you when you visit her next time. . . ."

I did not find the *cuento* of *La Cenisosa* in the Paterson Public Library, nor in any other book collection for many years. Recently, I ran across an anthology of *cuentos folkloricas* from Puerto Rico, and there it was: *La Cenisosa*. In *La Cenisosa* of Puerto Rico, Cinderella is rewarded by a family of three *hadas madrinas,* fairy godmothers, for her generosity of spirit, but her prize is not the hand of a prince. Instead she is rewarded with diamonds and pearls that fall from her mouth whenever she opens it to speak. And she finds that she can be brave enough to stand up to her wicked stepmother and stepsisters and clever enough to banish them from her home forever.

● ● ● ● ● ●

BRITNEY SPEARS

Singer, dancer

born: 1981

WHO SHE IS:

After two attempts the superstar Britney Spears became a member of the Disney Channel's Mickey Mouse Club at age eleven. By the time she was seventeen, Ms. Spears was a household name, topping the music charts with her number-one album, . . . *Baby One More Time.* Her second album, *Oops! . . . I Did It Again,* sold over 1.3 million copies in its first week out. The Britney Spears Foundation, created with the Giving Back Fund, started a performing arts summer camp for under-privileged kids in New England.

*B*ritney Spears may be a huge star around the world, but at home in Kentwood, Louisiana, she's just one of the gang hanging out with family and friends. This small town has supported her every move, including bringing in cable television just so they could watch their Britney on The Mickey Mouse Club. The people who know Britney best give her the security and strength to keep growing. After taking her show on the road, Britney knows she can always go home again to loving relationships.

❧

My hometown is the kind of place where everyone knows everyone else—people honk their horns and yell "Hi, y'all!" when they pass you on the road. (Although Mama will tell you they're honking their horns at me because I'm a bad driver!) They'll stop you on the street to ask you how you did on your geometry test. There's a real feeling of pride and kinship in our little town, and people look out for one another. I love everything about my home, except maybe for one little thing: everybody knows everybody's business.

You can imagine what happened when I started going around and doing talent competitions and auditioning far away in big cities like New York; well, we were quite the buzz over at the City Cafe. Everyone had an opinion about it. Some even thought my family was crazy.

Other folks, however, thought it was great and really cheered me on—especially when I did finally get to be a Mouseketeer when I was eleven. (The second time must be the charm.) Practically the whole town turned out to send me and Mama off to Orlando, where the show was taped. They all had "Britney Spears Fan Club" T-shirts that they made up specially for me, and they had a huge cake. They even declared it the official Britney Spears Day in Kentwood. Now, you know you wouldn't find that in a place like New York or L.A., but in a small town you're a family.

Today, my friends from Kentwood—Laura Lynne,

Elizabeth, Jansen, Cortney, Wendy, Erin, and Cindy—are still my best friends in the world, and we make sure we stay in touch (writing, calling, visiting, you name it). These are the girls I was in day care and dance lessons with—we just go way back. I know a lot of people who lost touch with their friends when they got all wrapped up in show business. Well, that's like losing touch with who you are: I don't care how busy you are—you make time for the people who mean a lot to you. That goes for family, that goes for friends. It doesn't take but a minute to call up and say, "Hey, what y'all up to?"

• • • • • •

JACKIE JOYNER-KERSEE

Track and field Olympic and world record champion

born: 1962

WHO SHE IS:

Jackie Joyner-Kersee is an Olympic champion who has become the fastest, and the longest- and highest-jumping female athlete in track and field to date.

Jackie Joyner-Kersee was only ten years old in 1972, when Title IX, the legislation mandating equal access for boys and girls to sports in school, became law. After its passage her basketball team was able to get the *same court time as the boys', but other battles still needed to be won. Jackie's coaches fought those battles, and because of their commitment Jackie's team was able to experience all the great aspects of playing sports—meeting people, competing fairly, and, of course, winning. It was Jackie Joyner-Kersee's coaches who extended her a helping hand.*

৯৯

At a very young age I was exposed to lots of sports, and I was eager to try them all—track, basketball, dancing. Whatever our community center offered, I tried, figuring eventually I'd get good at one of them. I immediately loved playing basketball. That's when I noticed a big difference between boys' and girls' sports in junior high and high school. We had one gym, and the girls always had to practice sports after the boys, at six-thirty or seven at night. My parents weren't going to let me play because they were worried about my walking home after practice in the dark. Eventually, attitudes changed and people started taking us seriously, especially after we won State in basketball and track.

Then the following year, Title IX passed and the system changed. A lot of people still didn't follow the law, but we had coaches that would fight for us and really started using the law to our advantage. We didn't realize all the challenges that existed because our coaches protected us from the race and sex issues. We were only slightly aware of it, but I know it affected our coaches. They were always fighting for us. In some places, we couldn't get off the bus and we didn't know why.

The coaches' goal was to teach us to always be respectful, to go out there and play hard. We focused on what we could control. Much later, I realized all that we went through to play. I was so blessed to have people guiding us through that maze, because a lot of those things could have deterred me from what I really wanted to do. I credit our devoted coaches, because not only did they care about us as being great athletes but they also cared about us as being great people. Even though some people were bitter toward us, our coaches encouraged us to be friends with all people. They wanted us to travel throughout the Midwest and meet competitors from all over. It was a great opportunity, and we not only got along with everyone but had so much fun.

● ● ● ● ● ●

SIGOURNEY WEAVER
Actor

born: 1949

WHO SHE IS:

Sigourney Weaver, a graduate of the Yale Drama School, launched her screen career with the memorable role of Lt. Ellen Ripley in *Alien* and has since played in every sequel. Her versatile acting shines in films such as *Gorillas in the Mist* (she portrayed the primatologist Dian Fossey), *Ghostbusters, The Year of Living Dangerously, Dave, The Ice Storm,* and *Galaxy Quest.* Ms. Weaver loves the theater and is also recognized for her numerous stage performances. When not acting she works with her production company to introduce new voices from the theater to the film industry.

Sigourney Weaver grew up in Manhattan and took the bus to grammar school every day until she transferred to an all-girls' boarding school. A week doesn't go by that she doesn't think about the English teacher in high school who made her feel so special. Her name was Florence Hunt. Unfortunately, this generous and kind woman died before Sigourney had the chance to thank her. Though she regrets this missed opportunity, Sigourney remains grateful for the gift given by Florence Hunt.

❧

I worked hard as a student, but I was not very focused when I was younger. I was fortunate to go to a wonderful all-girls' boarding high school in Connecticut called the Ethel Walker School, where I met my teacher, Florence Hunt. Miss Hunt taught English, and I had her for the last two years I was there. For some reason, Miss Hunt saw a lot of promise in me. I would say things like "I don't think Hamlet is the most interesting person; I think a play should be written about Claudius because he's in the most trouble." Most teachers would roll their eyes at these kinds of ideas, but Miss Hunt never did. She really listened and made me feel like I had an interesting mind and a unique perspective.

She often took me to the theater in Hartford, Connecticut; just the two of us would go on Saturday afternoons. I was thrilled to be introduced to new ideas. I had lots of creative impulses, and she always encouraged me to channel them and write plays. She gave me a kind of legitimacy I could never give myself.

After my graduation from college and Yale Drama School, I returned to my high school to see her. I wanted to thank her for all she'd done for me, but I was too late. She'd already passed away. To this day, I regret not visiting her sooner. I cannot stress how much she did for me in terms of self-esteem and my expectations for myself. I don't think anyone had expected that much of me, or if they had I was completely oblivious to it. Florence Hunt was a wonderful teacher who gave me a great gift. Every student should be fortunate enough to have someone who really identifies and understands his or her specialness. It helps the student ignite into the person she's going to be. She's no longer here, but there are other teachers like Florence Hunt out there. We all have the potential to be a Florence Hunt is how I look at it.

● ● ● ● ● ●

ELEANOR ROOSEVELT
U.S. First Lady, writer, humanitarian
1884–1962

WHO SHE IS:

Known throughout the world for her devotion to human rights, Eleanor Roosevelt was the first wife of a president to take an active role outside the White House. She fought fearlessly for the rights of the poor, women, children, and African-Americans.

*B*orn into an aristocratic family, Eleanor Roosevelt *appeared to have everything a girl could want. Yet by the time she was ten, both her parents and her younger brother had died. She delved into a fantasy life, constantly reading books and preferring to be alone. Many aunts doted on Eleanor, and she especially loved the companionship of her aunts Maude and Pussie, who* *exposed her to literature and the arts. With very few friends her own age, Eleanor sought out older women. One in particular, a family friend named Alice Kidd, was attentive and genuinely interested in what Eleanor had to say. Of her Eleanor says, "She was a great influence on me in these early years."*

༚

I thought her one of the most beautiful and certainly one of the kindest people I knew as a child, and if she was expected, I would walk half a mile or more to our entrance for the pleasure of driving in with her and seeing her before she was swallowed up by the older people. I was a little self conscious about this devotion and I doubt if she ever knew or if any of the others knew how much I admired her and how grateful I was for her rather careless kindness. But I learned something then, which has served me in good stead many times—that the most important thing in any relationship is not what you get but what you give. It does not hurt to worship at a shrine which is quite unconscious, for out of it may grow an inner development in yourself and sometimes a relationship of real value. In any case, the giving of love is an education in itself.

● ● ● ● ● ●

COKIE ROBERTS

Broadcast journalist, author

born: 1943

WHO SHE IS:

Cokie Roberts is chief congressional analyst covering politics, Congress, and public policy for both ABC News and her weekly television show, *This Week with Sam Donaldson and Cokie Roberts.* She is also a news analyst for National Public Radio and author of *We Are Our Mothers' Daughters,* a book highlighted by personal anecdotes that addresses significant issues facing women today.

*E*ven though Cokie Roberts thrives on covering current events for national television, she treasures nurturing her family and friends at home. Those times bring Cokie her back to her childhood—being surrounded by relatives and friends at the dinner table, listening to conversations, taking in bits and pieces. Of the many who have influenced Cokie's life, most have been women: aunts, grandmothers, and other mothers who fussed and guided and shared with her their special prescriptions for living a good life.

༺༻

The relationship to an adult not your parent can be one of the best in life. Aunts, uncles, grandparents,

great-aunts and -uncles, courtesy aunts, and uncles—
all made such a difference in my life. When I was growing up, we lived part of the year in New Orleans, part
of the year in Washington, so it had the feel of a some-
what schizophrenic childhood. In Louisiana, family surrounded me. My mother was an only child, but her
mother sometimes lived next door with two of her sisters and their mother. Six blocks away was my mother's
first cousin Shingo, not an actual aunt, but considered
one, what we call a "tante." Her daughters were just on
either side of me in age. Though I found my own house
fascinating with its mix of politicos from all parts of
town and every ethnic background, it was sometimes
a relief to skip the six safe blocks to a world with
backyard swings and midday snacks. I loved stuffing
envelopes at our dining room table with the campaign
volunteers; it made me feel wonderfully competent to
be able to fold the election flyers with the best of
them. And I listened to all the conversation about
issues and intrigue.

The men in this universe of adults often charmed
and delighted us, but they were mostly drop-ins on our
lives. It was the women we spent time with, it was from
them that we learned about generations, about how
things used to be, and how things would forever be.

● ● ● ● ● ●

KIM NG

Professional baseball executive

born: 1968

WHO SHE IS:

Kim Ng is vice president and assistant general manager of the New York Yankees. As one of only a few high-ranking females in professional baseball, Ms. Ng oversees day-to-day operations and negotiates contracts for the players. She previously worked for the Chicago White Sox, where she began as an intern after graduating from the University of Chicago.

Kim Ng is most comfortable wearing jeans and a pair of sneakers. She knows that what you look like on the outside has nothing to do with the person you are on the inside. She learned this from the older women in her life—her mother, her aunts, and her grandmother—who taught by example. Another role model was the tennis champion Martina Navratilova. By watching Martina in action Kim Ng gained the confidence to believe in herself.

❧

I loved to play most sports—softball, tennis, soccer, handball. I loved to play outside and go to movies. I collected baseball cards, and I liked to keep scrapbooks of all my favorite things. And when I was a kid, believe it or not, my favorite baseball team was the Yankees. But if you asked me who my idol was, her name is Martina Navratilova. She was the number-one tennis player in the world for many years. I didn't like her just because she was the best. I liked her because she changed the way the game was played. She changed the way women tennis players thought of themselves, the way they prepared for the game. Because they wanted to keep up with Martina, they had to become more fit, had to start running and lift weights, had to think about nutrition. She created a new standard. Martina was also outspoken in her beliefs and promoted women's tennis relentlessly. She was a true leader on and off the court. By watching her, I realized it was okay to be different. That has been my fuel for many years—it's okay to be different. I am comfortable and secure with who I am. It's important to believe in yourself and what you stand for. And when you've found all this stuff out—when you love something and you believe in it—you need to do whatever you can to help the cause. If we all care a little bit less about what other people think, it's going to help us in the long run.

• • • • • •

HELEN KELLER

Advocate for the deaf and blind

1880–1968

WHO SHE IS:

Helen Keller was the first blind and deaf person to communicate effectively with the sighted and hearing world. With the help of her lifelong teacher, Anne Sullivan, Ms. Keller learned how to communicate through her hands, read Braille, and eventually speak. She graduated from Radcliffe College—the first blind person to do so. Ms. Keller was a true visionary for the disabled and single-handedly changed how the world perceives them. She also learned to speak several languages.

Perhaps there is no more famous relationship than that between Helen Keller and her extraordinary teacher, Anne Sullivan. When Helen was nineteen months old an illness left her deaf, blind, and mute. She became a wild child trapped in her body, not knowing how to express her emotions. Anne Sullivan, who had once been blind but had her vision restored through two operations, was chosen to help Helen. Through sheer willpower and persistence, Anne was able to get through to Helen and unleash her remarkable talents. Anne started by teaching Helen how to use her fingers to spell words and then sentences. Trust was the main ingredient in this powerful relationship. Teaching the names of things is one thing, but teaching abstract thought is quite another. Helen recalls the first time she understood the meaning of "love."

❧

I remember the morning that I first asked the meaning of the word, "love." This was before I knew many words. I had found a few early violets in the garden and brought them to my teacher. She tried to kiss me: but at the time I did not like to have anyone kiss me except my mother. Miss Sullivan put her arm gently round me and spelled into my hand, "I love Helen."

"What is love?" I asked.

She drew me closer to her and said, "It is here," pointing to my heart, whose beats I was conscious of for the first time. Her words puzzled me very much because I did not understand anything unless I touched it.

I smelt the violets in her hand and asked, half in words, half in signs, a question which meant, "Is love the sweetness of flowers?"

"No," said my teacher.

Again, I thought. The warm sun was shining on us.

"Is this not love?" I asked, pointing in the direction from which the heat came. "Is this not love?"

It seemed to me that there could be nothing more

beautiful than the sun, whose warmth makes all things grow. But Miss Sullivan shook her head, and I was greatly puzzled and disappointed. I thought it strange that my teacher could not show me love.

A day or two afterward I was stringing beads of different sizes in symmetrical groups—two large beads, three small ones, and so on. I had made many mistakes, and Miss Sullivan had pointed them out again and again with gentle patience. Finally, I noticed a very obvious error in the sequence and for an instant I concentrated my attention on the lesson and tried to think how I should have arranged the beads. Miss Sullivan touched my forehead and spelled with decided emphasis, "Think."

In a flash I knew that the word was the name of the process that was going on in my head. This was my first conscious perception of an abstract idea.

For a long time I was still—I was not thinking of the beads in my lap, but trying to find meaning for "love" in the light of this new idea. The sun had been under a cloud all day, and there had been brief showers; but suddenly the sun broke forth in all its southern splendour.

Again I asked my teacher, "Is this not love?"

"Love is something like the clouds that were in the sky before the sun came out," she replied. Then in simpler words than these, which at the time I could not have understood, she explained: "You cannot touch the clouds, you know; but you feel the rain and know how glad the flowers and the thirsty earth are to have it after a hot day. You cannot touch love either, but you feel the sweetness that it pours into everything. Without love you would not be happy or want to play."

The beautiful truth burst upon my mind—I felt that there were invisible lines stretched between my spirit and the spirit of others.

SIGNIFICANT FIRSTS

❧

Experiences That Form Who We Are

First-time feelings of joy, fear, success, and even frustration help define who we are. First experiences at this age sometimes hit with a wallop. The end result is not always what you expected, but each attempt to venture out and try something new contributes to forming opinions, passions, and identity. Your physical self is certainly experiencing many firsts: your first period, first feelings for romance, first awareness of your body changing. It could be your first opportunity to go away on a class trip or with a friend's family. Try it. You might like it. You could have the chance to experience something you've only dreamed about, like trying a new sport or musical instrument, or training for a new after-school job. Try it, you might not like it. It's all about taking chances, making some mistakes and learning from them.

Find peace in reading about these women's reactions to their own firsts—the first time they felt loneliness, the first time they recognized evil in the world, the first time they realized their potential, the first time they heard "No, you can't" and responded with "Yes, we can." The experiences shared here help describe universal feelings we all share. Check out Maya Angelou's poem "Human Family." We are from different races, generations, and cultures, but the human family has more similarities than differences. Your significant firsts are part of your growth. Gain knowledge and courage from these firsts and you will be on your way to becoming a stronger, more enlightened adult.

❧

Character cannot be developed in ease and quiet. Only through experiences of trial and suffering can the soul be strengthened, vision cleared, ambition inspired and success achieved.

Helen Keller

CANDICE Actor
BERGEN born: 1946

WHO SHE IS:

Candice Bergen is best known for her performance on the award-winning TV sitcom *Murphy Brown*, where she played the title role, an outspoken and opinionated news anchor. She was born into Hollywood aristocracy, daughter of the famous radio host and ventriloquist Edgar Bergen. She began acting in movies in 1965. She is also an accomplished photojournalist and wrote her memoir, *Knock Wood*, in 1984.

For Candice Bergen, growing up in California meant balmy weather, convertibles, and movie stars. One day Candice's dream came true when her movie star idol sailed up to her parents' beach house. Candice had only fantasized about the man on her bedroom poster. Now a little innocent flirting led to a secretly arranged date. Be careful what you wish for. Candice's dreams turned into a scary reality when she quickly realized she was in way over her head.

ฌ

I lowered myself out the window, down the vine and darted, crouched like a commando, from palm to palm, zigzagging across the driveway in a bid for cover.

His big black car hovered like a giant manta ray out of the circle of street lamps. As I came alongside, the door swung open: a Cadillac convertible.

I slid across the smooth upholstery, banging my knee on something and sending it clattering. "Oh, a phone!" I exclaimed (relieved at such a handy conversation piece). "You have a phone in your car?"

"In case the studio needs to reach me," he said, replacing the receiver in its cradle while I nodded sagely, wondering what to say next. But he was talking as he headed the car toward Sunset, climbing Coldwater Canyon, crossing Mulholland, and coasting down into the Valley below.

"How's school?" he asked. Did I have many boyfriends? I bet he had a lot of girlfriends, though. But he laughed and said no, no girlfriends. At the moment, he had alimony payments—and his second wife was suing him for divorce. No, he laughed, no girlfriends. Lucky for me, I thought. Who would be dumb enough to divorce him? How old was he, if he didn't mind? He was staring straight ahead. Thirty-six, he said, turning off onto a dirt road that led into a citrus orchard, down through groves of orange and grapefruit trees. Thirty-six.

"My farm," he said, reading the question in my expression. "I bought it as an investment last year. Land is gold, Kiddo, didn't your father tell you that?"

He switched off the ignition and smiled at me. His teeth seemed to glow in the dark. Face flushed with shyness and excitement, eyes locked on my loafers, the careful cuffs of my jeans, the soft rolls of my socks; heart racing with forbidden feeling, with love, with fear, with the romance of it all. For this man's hands were touching me now, pulling me to him, and he was kissing me.

A light rain was beginning to fall, pulling the California grapefruit off the trees to land with soft thuds on the convertible. This was now, heading into deeper, darker waters, and I was trying to keep from going under. In one night, I had gone from fourteen-year-olds in white bucks and braces to thirty-six-year-old movie stars in cashmere and real estate. From guys in letter sweaters to men in divorce suits. I was in way over my head.

He got rougher and more persistent as I knocked the mobile phone from its cradle once more in a hasty retreat across the seat. My back flattened against the padded Naugahyde door; he came at me, talking softly, firmly, asking me what was the matter? What was I afraid of? Didn't I realize how many women would love to be in my place? Yes, I did, I nodded, thinking how much I wished they were.

I became frightened as he began to lose patience, my mind searching for simpler, safer things. I had no idea where he had taken me, but, suddenly, I knew where I wanted to be: home, Auntie Em. Back in my bedroom with the horse-show ribbons and petrified prom gardenias, my sailing trophy and my stack of 45s. Back in my canopy bed by the soft glow of my beloved clock radio. Home safe in my new teenager's room.

I had persisted in playing it as a game when it had clearly never been one, and finally fed up with my "childish attitude," he soon agreed that I belonged back with my record collection, not with him.

We drove home in stony silence. I felt ashamed, relieved, apologetic. As we approached my house, all he said was, "I wouldn't mention this to your parents, okay? They might not approve." Mention it to my parents? Might not approve? Was he insane? Was I?

We pulled up a discreet distance from the house. He reached across me to open the door. "So long, sailor." "So long," I said, and ran up the driveway, tunneled under the ferns and hoisted myself in through the window. Changing into my nightgown, I crept out from my room to check: the housekeeper dozed in the den in front of the television. All quiet on the home front. I burrowed under the covers, snug in my bed, turning my clock radio on softly, soothed by the music, safe in its glow. My room. My radio. My, my, my. Home, sweet home.

● ● ● ● ● ●

ESMERALDA SANTIAGO

Writer

born: 1948

WHO SHE IS:

Esmeralda Santiago is a renowned writer whose works include two autobiographies, *When I Was Puerto Rican* and *Almost a Woman.* Both explore the difficulties of merging two cultures. She has written one novel, *America's Dream,* and also produces documentary films.

Esmeralda Santiago knows firsthand about change. When she was thirteen she and her ten younger brothers and sisters moved from Puerto Rico to Brooklyn, New York, their single mother leading the way. Once she learned a new language and culture, life changed drastically for Esmeralda. Though she adapted quickly to her new life, her mother resented the changes and tried to slow down the process. Esmeralda did not have an easy time adapting to people categorizing her by race. She didn't like it at all.

❧

I was neither black or white; I was triguena, wheat-colored. I had "good" hair, and my features were neither African nor European but a combination of both. In

Puerto Rican schools, my skin color or features didn't make me stand out. I was never the darkest or the lightest in a room. But when we moved to Brooklyn, I was teased for being a jibara from the country. When I'd return to Puerto Rico, my city experience made me suspicious of others. . . .

I wanted a different life from the one I had. I wanted my own bed in my own room. I wanted to be able to take a bath without having to shoo the whole family out of the kitchen. I wanted books without a date due. I wanted pretty clothes that I chose for myself. I wanted to wear makeup and do my hair and teeter on high heels. I wanted my own radio so that I could listen to La Lupe on the Spanish station or Cousin Brucie's Top 40 countdown on the American one. I wanted to be able to buy a Pepsi or a Baby Ruth any time I craved one. In Puerto Rico, I hadn't wanted any of those things, didn't know they were in my reach. But in Brooklyn, every day was filled with want, even though Mami made sure we had everything we needed. Yes, I had changed. And it wasn't for the better. Every time Mami said I had changed, it was because I had done something wrong. I defied her, or was disrespectful, or didn't like the same things as before. When she said I had changed, she meant I was becoming Americanized, that I thought I deserved more, that I was better than anyone else, better than her. She looked at me resentfully, as if I had betrayed her, as if I could help who I was becoming, as if I knew.

● ● ● ● ● ●

ANNE FRANK
Writer, Holocaust victim

1929–1945

WHO SHE IS:

Anne Frank became famous after the publication of her remarkable journal, *The Diary of Anne Frank.* The book chronicles the dreams and frustrations of this young girl hiding from the German Nazis.

Anne Frank's heart ached with loneliness. Before her life turned upside down, she led a typical teenage life in Amsterdam. She liked school but yearned for a best friend to whom she could confide. On her birthday Anne was given her first journal, which turned into a depository for her feelings and so became like a friend. She wrote in it when she felt lonely and depressed. A month after Anne wrote this entry, her family moved to their secret annex.

❧

Now I'm back to the point that prompted me to keep a diary in the first place: I don't have a friend. Let me put it more clearly since no one will believe that a thirteen-year-old girl is completely alone in the world. And I'm not. I have loving parents and a sixteen-year-old sister, and there are about thirty people I can call friends. I have a throng of admirers who can't keep their adoring eyes off of me and who sometimes have to resort to using a broken pocket mirror to try and catch a glimpse of me in the classroom. I have a family, loving aunts and a good home. No, on the surface I seem to have everything, except my one true friend. All I think about when I'm with friends is having a good time. I can't bring myself to talk about anything but ordinary everyday things. We don't seem to be able to get any closer, and that's the problem. Maybe it's my fault that we don't confide in each other. In any case, that's just how things are, and unfortunately they're not liable to change. This is why I've started the diary. To enhance the image of this long-awaited friend in my imagination, I don't want to jot down the facts in this diary the way most people would do, but I want the diary to be my friend, and I'm going to call this friend Kitty.

● ● ● ● ● ●

NINA Broadcast journalist
TOTENBERG born: 1944

WHO SHE IS:

Nina Totenberg is the award-winning legal affairs correspondent for National Public Radio and can be heard regularly on *All Things Considered, Morning Edition,* and *Weekend Edition.* She covers the U.S. Supreme Court, making the legal arguments comprehensible. Ms. Totenberg also writes frequently for major newspapers and magazines.

Nina Totenberg wanted to be a journalist from an early age. She stuck by that decision and today often breaks important news stories. Nina was a true pioneer in broadcast journalism, among the first women to enter that field. Though she felt the sting of sexual discrimination, her threshold for pain was high, high enough to make things happen for herself and pave the way for others. Read between the lines, says Nina. If you knock on a door and the answer is no, knock on another door.

☙

In high school I realized I wanted to be a journalist when this thought occurred to me: the best way to witness history in the making was by being a reporter. At age fifteen I passed out political literature, but that didn't cut it for me. I wanted the vantage point journalists have, a seat near center stage, where the drama of history unfolds. The only question was how to get there. During my first job interviews, I was astonished when people said they didn't hire women. In the mid-sixties there wasn't a Civil Rights Act yet, the word *sexist* wasn't even in the lexicon, and sexual discrimination lawsuits were unheard of, so it was tough. Today girls have so many options, some don't realize obstacles still block our paths—they just tend to be placed at a higher level. When young women do hit one, I've witnessed many of them crushed and enraged by the experience. My advice is, remember your goal. There are many battles in the workplace—it's important to pick the ones that count. If someone comments on your pretty dress and you find it offensive, I would chose not to say anything only because there are many more things to care about, like good assignments, equal pay, and not being sexually harassed. If the "pretty dress" comment leads to something more serious, then action is required, but be careful what you take on. The workplace is filled with problems—some gender-related, some not—learning how to chose battles worth fighting for is key.

• • • • • •

MAYA ANGELOU

Writer, poet, actress, producer, director

born: 1928

WHO SHE IS:

Maya Angelou was asked by President Clinton to read her poem "On the Pulse of Morning" at his inauguration in 1993. Among her many published books, her autobiography *I Know Why the Caged Bird Sings* may be the most recognized and is studied in classrooms around the world.

Maya Angelou is a Renaissance woman. She embraces all that life offers: she speaks five languages fluently, writes, dances, teaches, and performs. Maya's distinct voice speaks with passion, articulating what so many feel but don't know how to say. Her own life experiences saturate her work: from growing up in Stamps, Arkansas, through her journalism work in Africa to her devotion to the civil rights movement. Her poem "Human Family" reminds us of our differences but, more important, our similarities.

&

HUMAN FAMILY

I note the obvious differences
in the human family.
Some of us are serious,
some thrive on comedy.

Some declare their lives are lived
as true profundity
and others claim they really live
the real reality.

The variety of our skin tones
can confuse, bemuse, delight,
brown and pink and beige and purple,
tan and blue and white.

I've sailed upon the seven seas
and stopped in every land,
I've seen the wonders of the world,
not yet one common man.

I know ten thousand women
called Jane and Mary Jane,
but I've not seen any two
who really were the same.

Mirror twins are different
although their features jibe,
and lovers think quite different thoughts
while lying side by side.

We love and lose in China
we weep on England's moors,
and laugh and moan in Guinea,
and thrive on Spanish shores.

We seek success in Finland,
are born and die in Maine,
In minor ways we differ,
In major we're the same.

I note the obvious differences
between each sort and type,
but we are more alike, my friends,
than we are unalike.

We are more alike, my friends,
than we are unalike.

We are more alike, my friends,
than we are unalike.

• • • • • •

MARY **Singer-songwriter**
CHAPIN CARPENTER **born: 1958**

WHO SHE IS:

The guitarist and singer Mary Chapin Carpenter has a crossover appeal that reaches a universal audience. Her songs, a combination of rock, blues, country, and folk, capture the struggles and dreams of day-to-day life. Among her awards are five Grammys, two best female vocalist awards from the Country

Music Association, and best female vocalist from the Academy of Country Music.

As a child Mary Chapin Carpenter was painfully shy. Writing songs helped her express her lonely and insecure feelings. One of three sisters, she grew up in Princeton, New Jersey, preferring folk music to the musical tastes of her family, which ranged from classical and opera to rock and roll. Encouraged by her father to play in local clubs after college, she discovered a surprise. Her shyness vanished onstage. Not at first, but the more she performed, the less shy she felt.

❧

Growing up was hard for me. I was a pretty shy kid, and I didn't make friends easily. I had a fair amount of adolescent angst, and within all those emotions rose the roots of music. I discovered that music and songwriting was a way to express myself and overcome my shyness. I was seven years old when I picked up my mom's old folk guitar and started listening to records and learning songs by ear. I figured out chord patterns from music books, and this quickly became a favorite thing of mine to do. I sang and scribbled dreadful little tunes and loved every moment.

So music was always a part of me, but I felt like I always had an internal life that was removed from school. When I was there, the creative spirit in me never felt entirely comfortable or accepted. I always felt left out—never part of the cool group, never pretty enough, popular enough, or athletic enough. On a social level, school was tough.

So I'm still shy, and it is interesting to me that I chose this profession, or it chose me, where I am forced to go out onstage and sing my music to huge audiences. Maybe it is a subconscious desire to break my shyness. But at the same time I feel like one thing feeds something else. The introspection—that sense of isolation that shyness gives you—is the thing that gives me the inspiration to write. So I wonder if I can't have the music without the shyness.

• • • • • •

JANE GOODALL

Primatologist, National Geographic Society explorer in residence

born: 1934

WHO SHE IS:

In 1960 Jane Goodall arrived in Africa's Gombe Forest to study chimpanzees. Her findings have revolutionized our understanding of primate behavior. Her research revealed that chimpanzees have distinct personalities, that they are meat eaters, and that they use blades of grass as tools to pluck termites from a mound. Today the Jane Goodall Institute continues observing chimpanzees, and Dr. Goodall travels over three hundred days a year, speaking to audiences about her studies, preserving the environment, and spreading her primary message—that we must be respectful of all life and that every single person can make a difference.

Just as Jane Goodall's study of chimpanzees taught the world that primates are not so different from us, in her earlier life she learned that not all human beings are alike. Jane grew up in a seaside home in England during World War II. She remembers the presence of American soldiers, food and clothing rations, and hovering in air-raid shelters during bombing attacks. She also remembers vividly seeing news stories about the German concentration camps. They would be her first lesson in evil, the first time she realized what some people are capable of. The lesson left an indelible mark on her.

༄

When the war finally ended in Europe on May 7, 1945, the grim rumors about the Nazi death camps were confirmed. The first photographs appeared in the newspapers. I was eleven years old at the time, very impressionable and imaginative. Although the family would like to have spared me the horrifying Holocaust pictures, I had never been prevented from reading the newspapers and they did not stop me then. Those photographs had a profound impact on my life.

I could not erase the images of walking skeletons with their deep-sunk eyes, their faces almost expressionless. I struggled to comprehend the agony of body and mind these survivors had gone through, and that of all the hundreds of thousands who had perished. I still remember seeing, with shock, a photo of dead bodies piled on top of one another in a huge mound. That such things could happen made no sense. All the evil aspects of human nature had been given free rein, all the values I had been taught—the values of kindness and decency and love—had been disregarded. I can remember wondering if it was really true—how could human beings do such unspeakable things to other human beings? It made me think of the Spanish Inquisition, and all the medieval tortures that I had once read about. And the terrible suffering that had been inflicted on black slaves (I had once seen a picture of rows of Africans chained in the galleys, a brutal-looking overseer standing with an upraised whip in his hand). I began to wonder, for the first time, about the nature of God. If God was good and all powerful as I had been led to believe, how could He allow so many innocent people to suffer and die? Thus the Holocaust dramatically introduced me to the age-old problem of good and evil. This was not an abstract theological problem in 1945; it was a very real question that we had to face as the horror stories mounted.

• • • • • •

SHERYL SWOOPES

Olympic Gold Medalist, forward for the Women's National Basketball Association Houston Comets

born: 1971

WHO SHE IS:

Sheryl Swoopes, an Olympic Gold Medalist, is the leading scorer for the WNBA Houston Comets and often voted Most Valuable Player. The Comets have won three WNBA championships under her leadership. Sheryl is also the first female athlete to have a Nike basketball shoe—Air Swoopes—named after her.

*A*t age seven Sheryl Swoopes had no dreams of becoming a championship basketball player because little girls didn't play basketball. Except Sheryl did. From the first time she handled a ball, she loved the game. That love kept her on the court, even though she didn't *get much support. Improving daily, she continued to indulge her passion until her talents were noticed.*

❦

When I was little I always played basketball with the guys. My mom thought it was too masculine and that I would get hurt. No one thought I should play basketball. So it finally got to the point where the more people told me I shouldn't play, the harder I worked at it. I wanted to prove them wrong. I remember thinking, It's fun, I enjoy it, and I believe in myself, I know I can do this. There wasn't a Women's National Basketball Association when I was seven. I didn't think of it as my future. I just lived for the movement, day by day. At six or seven, it never registered that someday I would have the opportunity to play ball in college or even professionally. Nor did I care about that. I wanted to show people that I can do this. I felt that it was me against the world. No one believed in me or came over and said, "Okay, we see that you're not going to give up." I think after being told that you can't do something, you eventually start to doubt yourself, and at times I did. I remember thinking, Maybe I shouldn't be doing these things; nobody thinks I can or should, including my family, my brothers and my mom. But my desire to play basketball prevailed.

● ● ● ● ● ●

CYBILL SHEPHERD

Actress, model, singer

born: 1950

WHO SHE IS:

Cybill Shepherd's successful modeling and acting career began in the 1970s. She launched her acting career with her starring performance in *The Last Picture Show.* Her two hit TV series, *Moonlighting* and *Cybill,* won many awards and entertained millions. Her autobiography is called *Cybill Disobedience.* Cybill also enjoys singing and performs across the country.

Cybill Shepherd had to be coaxed into entering her first beauty pageant. On the day she won, she knew her life would change. Though her interests never revolved around her beauty, an accident made Cybill realize the high value her family placed on good looks.

❧

Even as I understood that beauty was armored protection in my family, a corseted thing that guaranteed my status as the perfect child, I seemed determined to imperil it with some regularity. I never saw the rusty filament of barbed wire sticking out of the vine-covered fence I was trying to scale on my Aunt Gwen's farm and didn't notice the blood pouring down the front of my new white vinyl snap-up jacket, only the pale look of horror on my mother's face when she saw the triangle of flesh dangling from my upper lip. It was my great good fortune that the doctor on call in the emergency room of the local county hospital refused to sew me up, recognizing that a plastic surgeon's hands were called for. I lay on the backseat of our station wagon with an ice pack until we got to Memphis and Dr. Lee Haines put over two hundred stitches into an area half the size of a dime. I went home with a huge dark lump crisscrossed with black thread. I remember crying as I looked in the mirror, my tears washing over the shiny, gooey salve that left a foul, medicinal taste in my mouth. But my own horrified reflection was no worse than the revulsion I saw on the faces of my parents and grandparents. I hid when the doorbell rang, sure that the neighbors were asking, "Whatever happened to that pretty girl?" It took three years for the scar to heal, leaving a faint triangular line below my nostrils. I learned an important lesson about the transience of beauty: in the blink of an eye, my unique family position was jeopardized. Disfigurement was not lovable. And I would never be perfect again.

● ● ● ● ● ●

BEVERLY CLEARY

Children's author

born: 1916

WHO SHE IS:

Beverly Cleary has written over thirty-five award-winning books about real-life kid adventures. Her memorable creations include the title characters in *Ramona the Pest, Henry Huggins,* and *The Mouse and the Motorcycle.* Ms. Cleary has sold over ten million copies of her books and receives more than one hundred fan letters a day.

By junior year in high school, Beverly Cleary was finally taking courses of interest to her: journalism, English, and French. Her father's new job alleviated stress at home, even though Beverly and her mother rarely saw eye to eye. Writing was Beverly's passion, and she was respected for her talent at school. When asked to write a school play, she was first honored and happy to gain support from her mother, then shocked to learn how cruel some girls could be.

&c.

Unexpectedly, something happened to take my mind temporarily off boys. Miss Burns, the chairman of the English Department, called me into her office and asked me, as president of the Migwan Club, to take charge of writing the script for the Girls' League Show, which was to raise money for a scholarship. All girls in the school automatically belonged to the league. She suggested Jane Welday, a bright girl with a sense of humor, as another writer. The show was to involve as many school clubs as we could work in. . . .

When the script was complete, Mrs. Graham, the biology teacher in charge of the production, said to me. "Beverly, you are just as pretty as the girls who get all the attention around this school. Miss Burns and I want you to play the leading lady."

I thought of myself as a plain girl with an unruly permanent wave, no lipstick, and a mouthful of glittering bands and wires, but now—well yes, thank you, Mrs. Graham, I would be delighted to play the leading lady.

As I walked home with Claudine, I was elated. No one had ever called me pretty before. I suddenly felt pretty. Pretty me! Pretty me!

This was one day I did not stop at Claudine's house. I hurried home to tell Mother; I telephoned friends. Mother, as pleased as I, told our next-door neighbor. "Good for you," everyone said. "It's time someone other than the same old clique received some attention."

Just before supper, the telephone rang. I answered. The call was from a girl prominent in Girls' League. Maybe some of the girls were becoming less snobbish, I thought. Then she said, "Some of us have been talking it over and have decided you should drop out of the show."

I had trouble believing what I was hearing. "How come?" I finally asked, my pleasure turning to bewilderment, and then to anger.

"Because you don't have the clothes to play the part," she informed me.

Bolstered by one of Mother's maxims from my childhood, "Show your spunk," I did not agree to withdraw. . . .

The curtain rose again. Applause. Bows. The eyeglasses of my parents twinkled from the center of the third row. Afterward friends and several boys I barely knew gathered to congratulate me.

The next week I received a formal note from the league thanking me for my contribution.

Pooh to you, I thought.

● ● ● ● ● ●

MARIAN ANDERSON
Opera singer
1897–1993

WHO SHE IS:

Marian Anderson is one of the great opera singers. She also played a pivotal role in our civil rights history. In 1939 Howard University asked Ms. Anderson to perform at Constitution Hall in Washington, D.C., but the Daughters of the American Revolution (DAR), owners of the hall, denied the request because of Marian Anderson's skin color. In protest, First Lady Eleanor Roosevelt resigned her DAR membership and arranged for Ms. Anderson to perform a concert at the Lincoln Memorial. Ms. Anderson was also the first African-American to sing for the New York Metropolitan Opera.

Marian Anderson will be remembered not only for her contralto voice but for her dignity and grace under pressure. As an African-American teen in the early 1900s, Marian witnessed prejudice and adversity firsthand. She was a treasured addition to her church choir and was encouraged to attend music school. But when she applied for admission, Marian discovered for the first time how ignorant and hateful others could be.

୨୧

I sensed the need for a formal musical education when I was in my teens and was beginning to make my first modest tours. I decided, in fact, to see if I could not go to a music school. I did not know whether we could afford it, but I thought that I ought to find out. Mother encouraged me, and so did other friends, but I had no idea where to turn until a person who had shown some interest in my problem suggested a school.

That music school no longer exists in Philadelphia, and its name does not matter. I went there one day at a time when enrollments were beginning, and I took my place in line. There was a young girl behind a cage who answered questions and gave out application blanks to be filled out. When my turn came she looked past me and called on the person standing behind me. This went on until there was no one else in line. Then she spoke to me, and her voice was not friendly. "What do you want?"

I tried to ignore her manner and replied that I had come to make inquiries regarding an application for entry to the school. She looked at me coldly and said, "We don't take colored." I don't think I said a word. I just looked at this girl and was shocked that such words could come from one so young. If she had been old and sour-faced I might not have been startled. I cannot say why her youth shocked me as much as her words. On second thought, I could not conceive of a person surrounded as she was with the joy that is music without having some sense of its beauty and understanding rub off on her. I did not argue with her or ask to see her superior. It was as if a cold, horrifying hand had been laid on me. I turned and walked out.

It was my first contact with the blunt, brutal words, and this school of music was the last place I expected to hear them. True enough, my skin was different, but not my feelings.

• • • • • •

IRENE O'GARDEN
Poet, author, performance artist

born: 1952

WHO SHE IS:

Irene O'Garden writes, performs, and teaches poetry. Her poetry appears in many literary journals and national magazines. Ms. O'Garden brings her work alive by performing her poems across the country. She is also a bookmaker and the author of two children's books.

To the artist Irene O'Garden weight is no laughing matter. She was a talented, kind-spirited, loving girl whose weight brought her much pain. In her book Fat Girl: One Woman's Way Out, *Irene gives an honest account of her relationship with food, the constant dieting and feelings of shame. But in the end she triumphs by realizing how important it is to love yourself no matter what you look like. In this stream-of-consciousness piece from* Fat Girl, *Irene expresses her deeply hurt feelings when she was the target of a very mean joke.*

❧

dear diary why are people mean Terry V my best friend we were even writing our book Fallen Angel already up to page ten together why would she do what she did tonight which was call me but it was a boy voice i didn't know whose. i took it in the basement by myself my thumpy heart. he said he saw me he said he liked me but just then mom called me to bring the groceries in so would he call me back o please o please. of course he would. at dinner i could hardly eat for once and then it rang and then my torture brother took it and would not get off until at last he did then it rang it was for me and it was him. i went down to the basement phone he said i was cute and would i go out with him and yesses pulsed all through me but before i spoke i thought how did he know me and where had he seen me and how could he know i make up for my horrible body by my good self and sense of humor wait hey wait who is this anyway giggles laughing in the background this is Terry's birthday and tonite the party i was not invited to i shouted great idea for your party Terry but i wasn't fooled i am not falling for it shut your crap traps all of you and slammed the phone as if it were my heart

• • • • • •

GLORIA STEINEM

Activist, writer, journalist

born: 1934

WHO SHE IS:

The writer and journalist Gloria Steinem has been at the forefront of the women's movement for over thirty-five years. She helped start two magazines, *New York* and *Ms.* magazine, where she is coeditor. She has also spoken on behalf of civil rights, gay rights, and the peace movement. Ms. Steinem's best-selling books are *Outrageous Acts and Everyday Rebellions* and *Revolution from Within*.

Gloria Steinem remained devoted to a mother whose mental illness she tried desperately to understand. The realization that her mother wasn't going to change forced Gloria to be more responsible than most girls her age. Hanging out with girlfriends and going to parties didn't occupy her time. Fixing dinner and cleaning the house did.

≈

For many years I also never imagined my mother any way other than the person she had become even before I was born. She was just a fact of life when I was growing up; someone to be worried about and cared for; an invalid who lay in bed with eyes closed and lips moving in occasional response to voices only she could hear; a woman to whom I brought an endless stream of toast and coffee, bologna sandwiches and dime pies, a child's version of what meals should be. She was a loving, intelligent, terrorized woman who tried hard to clean our littered house whenever she emerged from her private world, but who could rarely be counted on to finish one task. In many ways, our roles reversed: I was the mother and she was the child. Yet, that didn't help her, for she still worried about me with the intensity of a frightened mother, plus the special fears of her own world full of threats and hostile voices.

• • • • • •

KATHARINE GRAHAM
Newspaper executive

1917–2001

WHO SHE IS:

Katharine Graham was chairman of the executive committee and publisher of the *Washington Post,* the family newspaper she took over after her husband's suicide. Considered one of the most powerful women in America, Ms. Graham played a pivotal role in breaking two major news stories: publication of the Pentagon Papers, which revealed the United States' involvement in the

Vietnam War, and publication of the Watergate investigation, which became one of the greatest political scandals in American history. At age eighty Ms. Graham won a Pulitzer Prize for her autobiography, *Personal History.*

When Katharine Graham's family moved to Washington, D.C., from New York, she was enrolled at the Montessori school—a casual environment that encouraged her to learn at her own pace. She loved playing and reading, and avoided math at all costs. After third grade Katharine moved to the Potomac School, a private, conventional school that offered a much more rigid schedule. It was at Potomac, with the help of her gym teacher, where Katharine learned how to work well with others.

ॐ

My early dancing and acrobatics helped me athletically. By the fifth grade, I was fairly coordinated and had become proficient at team sports. Potomac was divided into two groups, the Reds and the Blues, which competed fiercely in games, races, volleyball, and other sports. I was on the red team and was inclined to be bossy, a trait of which I was quite unaware until Miss Preisha—the gym teacher, on whom I had a crush—pulled me aside one day and told me she thought I might be elected captain of the Reds if I didn't tell people what to do so much. Suddenly, I could hear myself egging people on or giving orders. I took her advice and, miracle of miracles, it worked! I became captain. This small triumph gave me great satisfaction. I had had my first social success, a sign that something was working.

• • • • • •

CAROL BURNETT
Television comedian, actress, singer

born: 1933

WHO SHE IS:

The actor, singer, and comedian Carol Burnett's Emmy Award–winning television show, *The Carol Burnett Show,* aired for over eleven years. Her comedic timing and originality in her sketches rank her as one of comedy's leading ladies. Ms. Burnett has performed on Broadway and has starred in various dramatic and comedic movie roles.

arol Burnett was raised in an impoverished Hollywood neighborhood, where she escaped her real-life drama at home by going to the movies. Both Carol's mother and father were alcoholics, so she lived with her grandmother, Nanny, who took care of her as best she could. In school Carol enjoyed lots of activities, including track and field, at which she excelled. At the age of fourteen she experienced her first serious schoolyard crush and decided to employ her athletic abilities to attract his attention. Her intention quickly turned sour.

ॐ

There was one area where I could outshine the rest of the girls at Le Conte: I could run. Our gym teacher, Mrs. Foal, had even written Nanny a note asking permission to coach me after school but Nanny had refused because she believed running was bad for the heart. There went my career in the Olympics, I thought.

It didn't stop me from challenging anyone and everyone in school to a foot race. I got a little bit of attention at first, but after a year or so my fleet-footedness became old news. Most of the girls had reached the conclusion that the way to catch a boy was to hold still, look pale, and act helpless.

As much as I thought I wanted to be able to do all those things, I couldn't pull it off. So I kept on running.

There was a new boy in school, a ninth grader, Joey. He was Italian, and he made the girls drool. The guys liked him, too, because he was a sensational athlete. Even though, in my heart of hearts, I still loved Tommy, my old boyfriend, I developed a side crush on Joey. My friend Norma was nuts about him, too.

His dad owned a liquor store in Burbank, and sometimes on Saturdays Norma and I would take the bus

(which I hated) and hang around talking to him all afternoon while he bagged merchandise. We found out his
phone number and called him every night until his
mother answered and told us to cut it out. He started
to pay a little more attention to Norma in school, and
I became desperate so I challenged him to a foot race.
I figured that would make him look at me all right. He
would fall in love with me and ask me to run through
life with him, hand in hand. At last he would have found
the girl who could keep up with him.

At first he thought I was kidding, but I kept bugging
him to meet me after school. He finally said okay. There
was an alley right next to the athletic field where a lot
of the guys and Judy, with the big bosom, hung out
round three o'clock every day and smoked cigarettes. It
was a block long and perfect for a race.

Norma, Ilomay, and I showed up around two minutes after the three o'clock bell and tried not to stare
too hard at the bad kids, who were already lighting up
in the alley. They cleared the way when Joey showed up.
"Hey, what's goin' on?" Judy took a deep drag and eyed
Joey up one side and down the other. She looked like
Ida Lupino in *Road House.*

"Don't ask me," Joey said. "This is all her idea." He
looked at me and then through me. "C'mon, let's get
this over with. I gotta get home."

Ilomay said, "all right . . . get ready . . ."

There we were, side by side—Joey and me—bent over, touching shoulders . . .

"Get set . . ."

My neck was throbbing. I pictured a perfect photo finish and him hugging me and saying, "Hey, you're really something!"

"Go!"

He tore up the alley like Superman, and it was over. I was left way behind, eating dust. He never even came back. I guess he ran right to the Burbank bus.

A couple of weeks later he asked Norma to go out.

● ● ● ● ● ●

RITA DOVE
Poet, novelist, educator
born: 1952

WHO SHE IS:

Rita Dove is the youngest person and the first African-American to hold the post of United States poet laureate, from 1993 to 1995. She is a professor of English at the University of Virginia.

Rita Dove's parents were well educated and encouraged her to excel. In her high school senior year, she was a Presidential Scholar at the White House, ranking as one of the year's top high school students. The library once refused to let Rita check out a risqué novel because of her age. Frustrated, Rita told her parents. They promptly wrote a note to the library stating she was allowed to read any book. Knowing her parents trusted her judgment gave Rita a sense of empowerment. She loved reading and discovered that food played a creative role with each new book she read.

▼

As a child, reading was very physical for me—I really felt I was chewing my way through the book. I also associated reading with eating in that I would take snacks and match them to books. The summer I was twelve, I decided to read all of Shakespeare—I didn't make it—but when I began to read the plays, I found I couldn't read them in one sitting so I would have to get snacks. I remember going through *Macbeth* and thinking it was so dark and bleak that I should only eat toast or dried bread, nothing extravagant. I got pulled so deeply into that world that I wanted to feel a little like it, too. I was trying to engage all my senses. So it became a kind of game: what snack am I going to eat when I read *Romeo and Juliet*?

▼

For Rita Dove, television watching was limited and trips to the library were a family ritual with only one rule to follow: Whatever books Rita checked out, she had to read. No problem. Each time she opens a book, her own world slips away as she meets new people and travels to unexpected places. Her poem "The First Book" introduces this feeling.

❧

THE FIRST BOOK

Open it.

Go ahead, it won't bite.
Well . . . maybe a little.

More a nip, like. A tingle.
It's pleasurable, really.

You see, it keeps on opening.
You may fall in.

Sure, it's hard to get started;
remember learning to use

knife and fork? Dig in:
you'll never reach bottom.

It's not like it's the end of the world—
just the world as you think

you know it.

● ● ● ● ● ●

PHOEBE ENG

Writer, activist

born: 1961

WHO SHE IS:

After practicing law in New York, Hong Kong, and Paris, Phoebe Eng founded *A. Magazine: Inside Asian America,* for the English-speaking, Western-oriented Asian market. She is the author of *Warrior Lessons: An Asian American Woman's Journey into Power* and lectures extensively on empowering women to be true to themselves. An award-winning social activist, Ms. Eng advises many national organizations on race relations. She was a member of the Ms. Foundation delegation to the 1995 UN World Conference on Women in Beijing.

Urged by her parents to "fit in," Phoebe Eng knew that was easier said than done. As a young girl Phoebe just wanted equal footing in school when fighting the usual teenage battles. She now sees "fitting in" as more of a coping mechanism, a survival tool. An innocent remark by one of her friends in high school stung deeply enough to make Phoebe realize that she was different.

৵৹

In the 1970s, in the Long Island suburb where we lived, multiculturism and diversity were pretty simple concepts. The motto was simple and basic: "Do whatever you can to be like everyone else, and you'll be absolutely fine." As in most suburbs and enclaves then and even now, "belonging" was the goal, and that meant differences had to be hidden at any cost, no matter how patent and indelible those differences might be. Deny your differences and they won't exist, my father would tell us back then. "You're just as American as anybody else," he'd say. And in enlightened times, perhaps he'd have been right. But back in the seventies it didn't explain why we were called chinks or why parents voiced polite concern at a PTA meeting when I was given the female lead in our high school bicentennial production of *Oklahoma!* implying that Asian Americanness was actually un-American.

I thought the rest of America, like my own town, was Jewish, and so Jewish was what I aspired to become. Our family must have been good at the assimilation game, since we were eventually jokingly dubbed the "Engsteins," a term of endearment and acceptance that must have meant: You are an honorary one of us. And because of this we do not notice your differences (really, we swear!). Even if we don't always understand your mom's heavy Chinese accent.

Our parents' regimen for ensuring that my sister and I became American allowed us certain privileges.

We were in essence the first Chinese American slackers. We didn't go to Chinese school on Saturdays like our cousins did, and we ate as much McDonald's as we wanted. We hardly ever ate Chinese food two days in a row, knowing that telltale clinging smell of Chinese food would be the scarlet letter of Chineseness once we stepped out of the house.

Jane Oberwager pulled into my driveway in her parents' wood-paneled Ford station wagon, packed already with Ilyse, Geri and Bonnie. With the Bay City Rollers blasting on WPLJ, Jane honked for me to join them, and like someone in a scene from *Happy Days,* I threw on my coat and hopped into the car, having just gobbled up the last mouthfuls of dinner that my mom had flash fried. We shot toward the city and Danceteria. It was Saturday night again.

The flash point came on the Long Island Expressway in the form of a harmless sentence. It was Bonnie, in her trademark follow-the-moment, don't-think-before-you-talk, endearing way, who blew my world apart.

"I smell Chinese food!" She took a short sniff to confirm it. The carload of us fell stone silent, as if Bonnie had said something vulgar and ugly and unmentionable, as if someone had farted or as if she had called attention to a friend's withered arm or a growth in the middle of my forehead. All eyes turned to me in my big rabbit fur coat.

It became very warm. I looked away and slowly rolled down the window to let out the warm, greasy smell of oyster chicken that clung to my coat and cut through the brittle winter air. I might wear the same clothes, paint my eyes larger, and have hair as big as any of them, but with Bonnie's tiny innocent statement the truth had been set loose. On a level so basic that the limbic sense of smell would suss it out, there was difference in me that I had learned to be ashamed of.

● ● ● ● ● ●

DORIS KEARNS GOODWIN
Writer, biographer, political commentator
born: 1943

WHO SHE IS:

Doris Kearns Goodwin worked with President Lyndon Johnson and assisted him with his memoirs. She is the author of four books, *The Fitzgeralds and the Kennedys, Lyndon Johnson and the American Dream,* the Pulitzer Prize winner *No Ordinary Time: Franklin and Eleanor Roosevelt: The Home Front in World War II,* and her memoir, *Wait Till Next Year.* Ms. Goodwin is a regular contributor to PBS's *The NewsHour with Jim Lehrer,* and she is also an expert on baseball.

*G*rowing up Catholic and a diehard Brooklyn Dodgers fan, Doris Kearns Goodwin had a storybook safe childhood, complete with living in a tree-lined neighborhood and her best friend next door. She enjoyed school and kept regular baseball stats, but Doris also had to watch the decline of her mother's health from severe heart problems. Because she couldn't lead an active life, Doris's mother found solace in reading, a love she passed on to her daughter. Her death when Doris was in high school left her daughter confused and devastated.

❧

The next morning, I woke at my usual hour—seven o'clock. In the first seconds, as I rolled onto my back to stretch, there was no recollection of what happened, and then every detail of the previous day flooded my mind—my first glimpse of my mother lying in bed, the startled expression fixed on her immobile face, the utter vacancy of my father's eyes, the grotesque intrusion of the men from the funeral parlor carrying the blanketed form down the stairs. No one was up yet. I wandered listlessly from room to room. I wanted my father, yet for the first time in my life, I was afraid to disturb him. I wanted to call my friends, but did not want to be pitied. I wanted it all to go away, but knew it wouldn't. The phrase "I am fifteen years old and my mother is dead" sounded repeatedly in my head. I went downstairs and looked at our family album, turning to the photograph I had loved which showed my mother in her early twenties, her legs hung over the arm of the chair. I felt bitter. It did not seem fair, so much pain and sickness in a life so short. It wasn't fair to me. Then I was ashamed. How could I think of myself now? It had been so much worse for her. Yet she never complained. And now she was dead. . . .

Although I understood my father's decision, I was sad, even resentful, at the prospect of leaving the only home I had ever known. The associations which compelled my father to leave only bound me more desperately to my home. For as long as I could remember, my sense of place, my past, my identity had been rooted in this house, this street, this neighborhood. Almost every memory I had of my mother was connected in some way or other to the house, to the rooms where she had been virtually housebound. I could picture her standing at the back door talking to the bakery man, reading in her favorite chair on the porch, ironing in front of the television, or cooking at the stove. I was afraid that when we moved these images would be left behind, that I would forget my mother.

● ● ● ● ● ●

SCHOOL RULES

❧

Some Lessons in Life

School rules in one way or another. The alarm clock rings and, blurry-eyed or not, you grab some toast and face another day. The daily grind has you lugging your backpack and rushing to geometry class. Yet it provides so much. School becomes your world, the backdrop to your life with friends, sports, and activities. It's your opportunity to shine, to achieve great grades and go out for the volleyball team. Indeed it's a challenge. Sometimes just figuring out what to wear can make or break your whole day. Never fear. There's always the next test, the next game, the next raging crush.

Like you, the women profiled here experienced both good and bad during their schooldays. Some had teachers who were crucial to their success. Some failed in one subject only to pass with flying colors in another. Some found peer pressure made school that much more difficult. Unfortunately, no one sees eye to eye with every teacher, and mean, unruly kids never seem to go away. Learning how to handle these situations is the only way to prepare you for life outside school. Ignore the bad stuff as much as possible. There are a lot of unhappy people out there—don't let them rain on your parade. Find an adviser who listens or buddy up with a pal who cares about you.

School is one big lesson in life. It's your first big journey outside home. It's the one place where you can start exploring all the different options available to you. Think of school as a palette full of great colors. Yes, reading, writing, and arithmetic are the backbones of your education, but seek out the zanier side of you. Sing in the choir, write for the newspaper, or master another language. You might discover a new you that thrives in the photography class darkroom or loves the applause you hear at the end of a performance. Enjoy the adventure, and oh yeah—make sure the dog doesn't eat your homework!

In the first grade, I already knew the pattern of my life. I didn't know the living of it, but I knew the line. . . . From the first day in school until the day I graduated, everyone gave me one hundred plus in art. Well, where do you go in life? You go to the place where you got one hundred plus.

Louise Nevelson

CAROL BURNETT

Television comedian, actress, singer

born: 1933

WHO SHE IS:

The actor, singer, and comedian Carol Burnett's Emmy Award–winning television show, *The Carol Burnett Show*, aired for over eleven years. Her comedic timing and originality in her sketches rank her as one of comedy's leading ladies. Ms. Burnett has performed on Broadway and has starred in various dramatic and comedic movie roles.

In her youth drama was Carol Burnett's thing. Always pretending to be her favorite movie actresses with her best friend, Ilomay, Carol decided to go for it and audition for the school play. This put her in front of the first audience that would cheer in response to her hilarious performance. Like many of life's experiences, this one, layered with happiness and sadness, ended traumatically for all involved.

❧

Reporting for the *Le Conte Junior High News* was one colossal bore. I wrote junk for the "Announcements" column. When I read what I wrote about the upcoming auditions for the ninth-grade senior play, I decided I'd try out for it myself.

The tryouts were being held in the school auditorium.

Mrs. McNeil, who was really one of the English teachers, doubled as the head of the drama department. She also wrote plays. For the ninth-grade effort that year she had selected one of her plays to produce.

It had a small cast. There was a father, a mother, a teenage daughter, her pain-in-the-butt kid brother, and a gum-chewing, wise-cracking maid, whose main function in life was to sass them all back. McNeil said her play was about a "typical family."

I set my cap for the part of Musie, the Maid. It wasn't the leading role, but she had the best lines, and she didn't have to look good. I popped two sticks of gum in my mouth to get into character and headed for the auditorium to give it a whirl. It looked as if every single senior in the whole school was there to try out for those five roles. When my turn came, I walked up the steps to the stage, opened the script, and started to read. Then I made the mistake of looking out into the audience. I saw the faces of the rest of the kids waiting for their turn. And they were glued to what I was doing. One of my ankles started wiggling. It wouldn't quit. I heard a very high, unfamiliar voice squeak its way out of my throat and proceed to crack, followed by an ear-shattering, body-quivering heartbeat, which also happened to be mine. At that very instant I knew what stage fright was.

I would've given anything to have turned into Claude Rains in *The Invisible Man* right then and there (please, God). No such luck. I was stuck. I was stuck right up there on stage, feeling naked as a jaybird, in front of the whole wide world, making a complete jackass of myself. Why, oh, why hadn't I stayed put in my journalism class, where I was safe and snug, writing my "Announcements" column? Better to be bored to death than scared to death.

McNeil barked out a direction: "Chew the gum harder!"

I did.

"Faster!"

I chewed so hard I thought I was going to dislocate my jaw. She kept me up there for what seemed like days. I thought that woman would never let up.

I finally heard the blessed word "Next!" and I bolted out the back door as fast as my weak pins could carry me. So much for acting. Better to be in the background, anyway. Directing maybe.

The next day I got a call-back.

How about that? Come to think of it, it really hadn't been all that awful. Even the pros admitted to a little stage fright, every now and then. It was only human. The second time around was a lot better. I made it a point this time not to look at the audience. I pretended to be the character, kind of the way Ilomay and I always did after we'd seen a movie. I even had some fun. I made faces and got laughs. Not bad, not bad at all. The role of Musie, the Maid was finally narrowed down to two of us: Gordon and me.

Gordon was a boy. He wanted to play Musie in girls' clothes. I'd never heard of such a thing. It was just plain stupid. A gimmick, that's what it was. And McNeil was falling for it! It wasn't fair.

Besides, Gordon was a weird kid. Strange-looking, with skin like Snow White, and hair not only black as ebony but fuzzy. He was forever clowning around with the kids on the field during recess, trying to get laughs, and he was forever falling flat. He ate celery and a pear every day for lunch, folded up his brown paper bag very carefully, and saved it.

Sometimes he'd look real pitiful, and when you felt sorry enough for him to say hi, he'd stare right through you. But usually you'd try to avoid him because if he got the chance, he'd pin you to your locker and shove joke after dumb joke down your throat until you pretended to laugh, just to break loose.

For some reason, Gordon was a favorite of McNeil's.

There was no question in my mind. He'd get the part. I walked around in a glob of gloom for three days. I had cast myself in a private play of my very own, a tragedy, and I was the star. They finally posted the chosen cast on the main bulletin board outside the principal's office.

I got the part.

So did Gordon.

There were going to be two performances, and we'd each get a crack at it. I'd get to play the first one, and he'd get to close.

We had a full house the Friday night we opened. I did okay. In fact, I was pretty good. I cracked my gum like crazy, made faces, hollered out my lines, and got laughs. I followed McNeil's direction to a T. Mama, Nanny, and Chrissy came and said they liked it a lot. Chrissy looked sleepy.

Backstage Ilomay, Norma, and the rest of our gang said they thought I stole the show. I wished like mad I could play it the next night, but it was over for me. All my buddies agreed I'd been gypped. I'd hardly got my feet wet. Well, let Gordon have his shot. I could afford to be gracious. I was a hit.

We all were in the audience Saturday night.

Gordon made his entrance, wearing Musie's maid uniform. The kids roared. Naturally. I mean, after all, he was a guy. The more they laughed, the less gracious I felt.

Then something started happening. He wasn't

Gordon in girl's clothes. He was Musie. He wasn't "act-ing" funny. He didn't have to. He just was.

And he was wonderful. He was so wonderful I forgot what I was feeling about myself, and when he came out to take his bow, all of us in the audience stood up and clapped and clapped.

Gordon became the campus star.

None of us could get it through our heads why, just weeks before graduation, he shot himself.

His picture was in the yearbook. It had been too late to take it out.

I started dreaming about him . . . almost every night there for a while. I dreamed we both were playing Musie at the same time. We were different from each other, but we were the same person, in the same body. I was Gordon, and Gordon was me. I'd tell him how sorry I was I'd ever been jealous of him, and I'd ask him where he'd be going after graduation, and he'd smile at me. He'd never talk, just smile. Then sometimes I'd see myself holding a gun, and the gun would disappear, and a whole bunch of people, who hadn't been there before, would stand up and clap and clap.

● ● ● ● ● ●

SYLVIA EARLE

Marine biologist, ocean preservationist, National Geographic Society explorer in residence

born: 1935

WHO SHE IS:

Sylvia Earle is a renowned scientist. She was leader of the first female team of aquanauts, she holds the world record for the deepest solo dive, and she is a protector of oceans. Dr. Earle has spent over six thousand hours submerged in the water. She has solved many underwater mysteries and discovered new species.

Sylvia Earle knows firsthand about what is happening to our oceans. Her study of marine life has come full circle, first discovering new species in the ocean and now watching some species become extinct. School answered her endless questions about the natural world around her. There weren't many girls interested in science in those days, but still Sylvia followed her passion and got into the thick of experiments and scientific studies whenever she could. If Sylvia couldn't be outdoors, she was just as happy to be learning in school.

I loved school. I was almost embarrassed at the time because you weren't supposed to love school, but I did. In some regards I didn't love the learning as much as I loved the chance to soak up everything. With my parents' encouragement, I always did well in school, and of course that makes a difference. I think that some children are sort of disadvantaged because school is looked upon as a luxury, not a necessity. Most parents don't take time, or cannot invest the time that my parents committed to me in terms of helping me learn, giving me an interest in reading and math. They were always there for me.

I had the additional benefit of guidance from my mother's sister, Aunt Karen, who was a schoolteacher and lived at home with us for many years. I also saw another aunt from time to time who was also a schoolteacher. My aunts first taught in one-room schoolhouses, when all classes were together, so they really understood the complexities of dealing with youngsters of many backgrounds, ages, and levels of confidence. I always loved books and reading. But it took me many years before I could understand the value of reading fiction. I devoured nonfiction books that I felt I could learn from. I understand now that you can learn a great many truths by telling a story, but I didn't understand that as a kid. I thought it was a waste of time.

I tended to be kind of out there by myself throughout all of school, partly because girls were not supposed to like science and I did. The classes that I took were with mostly guys. We were buddies, but I didn't form close relationships with them like women do with other women. It wasn't until after I got out of high school that I found friends that truly shared my close interest in nature and science.

When I was in the seventh grade, there was a teacher in the junior high school in Florida, Edna Tenure, who took an interest and encouraged my wayward ways. I love to draw, and I always drew animals of course and tried to figure out how things worked. She encouraged it. She gave me special projects because most of the kids just didn't care. They thought I was really weird.

● ● ● ● ● ●

BEVERLY CLEARY

Children's author

born: 1916

WHO SHE IS:

Beverly Cleary has written over thirty-five award-winning books about real-life kid adventures. Her memorable creations include the title characters in *Ramona the Pest, Henry Huggins,* and *The*

Mouse and the Motorcycle. Ms. Cleary has sold over ten million copies of her books and receives more than one hundred fan letters a day.

After Beverly Cleary graduated from college she became a librarian. Tired of reading children's books about poor kids who were saved by rich uncles, Beverly decided to fill the void and write fun stories that boys and girls could relate to. It worked. She stayed true to her mission—she never let money influence her writing and she did not follow trends. Beverly Cleary remains a traditional favorite among all kids. Her talent as a writer was obvious from the beginning.

ᏇᏉ

Next Miss Smith gave us homework: writing an essay about our favorite book character. This brought forth groans and sighs of resignation from most of the class. Nobody wanted to do homework, especially original homework. . . .

After I put together a Sunday dinner for my father, who gamely ate it and was enjoying his pipe and the Sunday paper, I sat down to write an essay. Which favorite character when I had so many? Peter Pan? Judy from *Daddy-Long-Legs*? Tom Sawyer? I finally solved the problem by writing about a girl who went to Bookland and talked to several of my favorite characters. I wrote on and on, inventing conversations that the characters might have had with a strange girl. As rain beat against the windows, a feeling of peace came over me as I wrote far beyond the required length of the essay. I had discovered the pleasure of writing and to this day, whenever it rains, I feel the urge to write. Most of my books are written in winter.

As much as I enjoyed writing it, I thought "Journey Through Bookland" was a poor story because the girl's journey turned out to be a dream; and if there was anything I disliked, it was a good story that ended up as a dream. Authors of such stories, including Lewis Carroll, were cheating, I felt, because they could not think of any other conclusion.

I was worried because I had used characters from published books. Miss Smith had lectured us on plagiarism and said that stealing from books was every bit as wrong as stealing from a store. But how could I write about a favorite character without having him speak?

When we turned our essays in during library, I watched anxiously as Miss Smith riffled through the papers. Was I going to catch it? Miss Smith pulled out a paper that I recognized as mine and began to read aloud. My mouth was dry and my stomach twisted up into a knot. She finished and paused. My heart pounded. Then she said, "When Beverly grows up, she should write children's books."

I was dumbfounded. Miss Smith was praising my story-essay with words that pointed to my future, a misty time I rarely thought about. I was not used to praise. Mother did not compliment me. Now I was not only being praised in front of the whole class but was receiving approval that was to give direction to my life.

● ● ● ● ● ●

WENDY WASSERSTEIN
Playwright

born: 1950

WHO SHE IS:

Wendy Wasserstein is the author of numerous Broadway plays, including *The Sisters Rosensweig* and *The Heidi Chronicles,* which earned her both a Tony Award and a Pulitzer Prize. Determined to give high school students more exposure to the arts, Ms. Wasserstein created her own theater program, which brings students to seven Broadway plays throughout the year. They keep journals on the experiences and earn academic credit.

Wendy Wasserstein's parents took her to a Broadway play almost every Saturday afternoon. That's when it

dawned on her that what you did for a living could coin-
cide with your real interests. Wendy's interests were the
arts. After discovering her dyslexia she turned to her cre-
ative side and excelled at school.

෨

I was an adolescent in Manhattan, which definitely gave me a false sense of sophistication, but it was a great place to explore. I have always been shy, which is why I write. I am a little bit awkward. I went to a small girls' school, and went to an all women's college, and that very much made its mark. That experience gave me a great sense of myself and taught me the importance of friends. I made some great friends along the way and still keep in touch with some from elementary school. I always knew I was funny, and that's how I got by. In high school we had mother-daughter fashion shows, and I knew nothing about fashion, but I knew they would excuse me from gym if I wrote those shows, so I did. They were big hits, very funny and full of songs and skits.

The best thing that can happen to you is to have a teacher who gives you confidence in your own voice. I had some good ones who I could talk to about ideas and concepts. I didn't confide in them about my personal life, but we discussed bigger issues, like communism, politics, and art.

I believe in very different ways of learning. I was diagnosed early as someone slightly dyslexic. Dyslexia had just come out, and in some ways I discovered it myself, because I could tell something wasn't quite right. I went to a reading institute, which helped, and then really felt at home in dancing school and became involved in plays—the arts meant a great deal to me. I am a big believer in arts education in the schools, because it encourages kids to look at education differently. The arts can expose subjects to some kids who might not understand them otherwise.

● ● ● ● ● ●

KATHARINE GRAHAM
Newspaper executive

1917–2001

WHO SHE IS:

Katharine Graham was chairman of the executive committee and publisher of the *Washington Post,* the family newspaper she took over after her husband's suicide. Considered one of the most powerful women in America, Ms. Graham played a pivotal role in breaking two major news stories: publication of the Pentagon Papers, which revealed the United States' involvement in the Vietnam War, and publication of the Watergate investigation, which became one of the greatest political scandals in American history. At age eighty Ms. Graham won a Pulitzer Prize for her autobiography, *Personal History.*

*G*rowing up in a house full of children, Katharine Graham was kept busy with a very active schedule. Music, French, riding, dance, and even posture lessons were part of her informal education. School provided her formal education. Fitting in with her peer group was left up to Katharine. At her new school, Potomac, finding a friend offered a comforting start.

❧

Entering Potomac as a new girl was difficult. I think of my life in my early years there as being solitary. I felt awkward, out of place, and different, especially in the ribbed socks that no one else wore. . . . Potomac proved to be my first big adjustment—one that helped me with a basic lesson of growing up: learning to get along in whatever world one is deposited. I had to observe what was done, to imitate. I had to cope with my loneliness, my differences, and become some other person. I was more or less alone until my second year there, or fifth grade, when I figured out how to start making friends by inviting people over to the house.

● ● ● ● ● ●

MARGARET BOURKE-WHITE

Photographer, photojournalist

1904–1971

WHO SHE IS:

Margaret Bourke-White was one of this country's first photojournalists. With a career that spanned over twenty-five years, Ms. Bourke-White earned many "firsts": she was the first photographer for *Fortune* magazine, the first Western photographer allowed in the Soviet Union, the first female photographer for *Life* magazine, and the first female war correspondent, entering combat zones during World War II. She also documented the concentration camps and was well known for her photographs of the Great Depression.

Margaret Bourke-White's house always bustled with creatures. Her parents tolerated her many insect projects and snake studies because they too were nature lovers. Margaret dreamed of traveling when she grew up and assumed she'd be a scientist, not a photographer. Her mother demanded the best from Margaret and always told her to "reject the easy path!" She fared well in school, but there was one thing missing in Margaret's life.

I went through school without getting something I passionately wanted. Throughout my grade-school and high-school days, I never was invited to a dance. Whatever the reasons, real or imaginary, my suffering was very real. I loved dancing: I danced around the kitchen with a dish towel when I was a youngster, and went to a dancing school when I was a little older. Mother said, "If you are a good dancer, you will always get dancing partners!" Then a dazzling event took place which I believed would change all that. It was unexpected as my faith in its influence was great. Plainfield High School, New Jersey, where I was then a sophomore, each year offered a prize "for excellence in literacy competition." The award was fifteen dollars in books to be selected by the winner, and the contest was open to the three upper grades. . . . When I learned that I had won first prize, my astonishment at my good fortune was less overwhelming than the radiant new future I saw opening up before me. The prize would be my passport to popularity. My career as a wallflower was at an end. Commencement exercises took place in the evening that year and were to be followed by a dance.

As couples paired up and dissolved into a swaying throng in the center of the auditorium, I took up my position confidently at the edge of the dance floor.

Throughout the foxtrot I stood serenely. Waltzes followed two-steps. One-steps followed waltzes. But not one boy—not one human in trousers—came up to ask me to dance.

Finally an older girl, a tall warmhearted friend of my sister's, came up and volunteered to dance. Here, on this night, to dance with a girl! This was the badge of failure. Through my distress I recognized her kindness; I could not refuse. I am sure that she, from the bottom of her generous heart, wished as fervently as I that we both could be stricken invisible.

• • • • • •

JACKIE JOYNER-KERSEE

Track and field Olympic and world record champion

born: 1962

WHO SHE IS:

Jackie Joyner-Kersee is an Olympic champion who has become the fastest, and the longest- and highest-jumping female athlete in track and field to date.

Jackie Joyner-Kersee might have made her athletic endeavors look easy, but behind her flawless skill was a determined young woman who worked hard for what she earned. For Jackie, bringing home good grades was the same as winning on the basketball court. She was successful at both.

❧

I challenged myself at school the same way I challenged myself on the track. I wanted to be able to bring home straight A's. I remember one time when I got all A's and an F in home economics. My father hit the warpath and wondered how I could get straight A's and then not pass home ec. Well, I couldn't cook, and I guess it showed, but when I saw my report card—that red F glaring at me—I decided that even though I might say "I can't" I will always find a way to say "I can." There was no way I could get A's in reading, spelling, English, and biology and not pass something as simple as home economics.

● ● ● ● ● ●

RITA DOVE
Poet, novelist, educator
born: 1952

WHO SHE IS:

Rita Dove is the youngest person and the first African-American to hold the post of United States poet laureate, from 1993 to 1995. She is a professor of English at the University of Virginia.

*O*ne of the youngest winners ever of the Pulitzer Prize for poetry, Rita Dove writes what she knows. Her poems come from her heart, her past, her ancestors' history. "Education is the key to doing whatever you want to do," said her father while Rita was in school. She read incessantly all year long, and the dictionary was her companion. In this poem Rita remembers her father's persistence in quizzing her on math.

❧

FLASH CARDS

In math I was the whiz kid, keeper
of oranges and apples. What you don't understand,
master, my father said; the faster
I answered, the faster they came.

I could see one bud on the teacher's geranium,
one clear bee sputtering at the wet pane.
The tulip trees always dragged after heavy rain
so I tucked my head as my boots slapped home.

My father put up his feet after work
and relaxed with a highball and The Life of Lincoln.
After supper we drilled and I climbed the dark

before sleep, before a thin voice hissed
numbers as I spun on a wheel. I had to guess.
Ten, I kept saying, I'm only ten.

● ● ● ● ● ●

PATRICIA POLACCO

Children's author

born: 1944

WHO SHE IS:

Patricia Polacco writes and illustrates books for children. She has published over twenty-five books, with many stories based on her own childhood experiences. Her titles include *The Keeping Quilt, Pink and Say, Chicken Sunday,* and *Rechenka's Eggs.*

Today Patricia Polacco travels to schools around the country reading her books and emphasizing the importance of arts education. Her devotion to the arts began in childhood. Because of her learning disabilities she was teased unmercifully by classmates. The experience left scars. Art offered her a way to escape from her learning-disabled world. Patricia believes all schools should enforce a no-tolerance rule on meanness.

❧

Not only did my teacher George Felker save my life, but so did art and drama. Drama was a place where I could turn into anyone I wanted to be, act out anything inside of me I couldn't figure out. Art is another language—like music, it's a language of the soul and heart. In my head, nothing held still, nothing was the same, there wasn't anything that I could count on other than my art. Then I was a ballet dancer, and dancing also meant everything to me. The arts are so important in adolescent life because they give you an opportunity to shine outside of school and your peer group; something you can point to and say, "I can do this very well." It could be anything, horseback riding, gymnastics, anything that interests you.

Adolescence is the time you really feel the strongest you will ever feel about issues, and this kind of enthusiasm should be embraced by kindness. Teasing is a really big deal to me. Hate is a crime now, and hate crimes start with hateful words. When we are indulged and allowed to use mean words on each other like weapons, it evolves into bigger crimes. The ultimate extreme of course is the Holocaust. How do you think it started? Someone feeling superior decided he was going to call somebody else mean names. It gained momentum from there. So for me, name-calling and feeling superior against other races and religions are pet peeves I like to talk about. I believe children are born loving and learn cruelty. They learn to hate and not always at school. Some kids learn it at home.

I applaud schools where meanness is not tolerated. I have been in schools where this no-tolerance policy is in place, and even though some say you can't legislate kindness, I beg to differ. In these schools, the children are encouraged to show generosity, kindness, and respect. School programs that mirror this image make these environments peaceful places to learn.

Not only was my early adolescence scarred by having terrible feelings about myself, which I think any fourteen-year-old does, but I was also the victim of one individual who was unmerciful in his teasing and use of unkind and hateful words. So much so that it started to erode my sense of well-being. As an adult, I realize that if someone is being unkind to you, they have a problem, but when I was a kid, I didn't have the ego strength to understand this. I shouldn't have believed what he said about me, but I did and it was devastating.

● ● ● ● ● ●

SIGOURNEY WEAVER
Actor
born: 1949

WHO SHE IS:

Sigourney Weaver, a graduate of the Yale Drama School, launched her screen career with the memorable role of Lt. Ellen Ripley in *Alien* and has since played in every sequel. Her versatile acting shines in films such as *Gorillas in the Mist* (she portrayed the primatologist Dian Fossey), *Ghostbusters, The Year* of Living Dangerously, Dave, The Ice Storm, and Galaxy Quest. Ms. Weaver loves the theater and is also recognized for her numerous stage performances. When not acting she works with her production company to introduce new voices from the theater to the film industry.

*S*usan Alexandra Weaver was slow to blossom. Tall and gangly at a young age, she was dissatisfied with not just her appearance but her name as well. At age fourteen, after reading The Great Gatsby, she changed it to Sigourney after a minor character in the book. What she did well was make people laugh, a skill that helped her find a place in her peer group at school.

๏

I was such a dork. I arrived at my boarding school at age eleven, and by then I had already reached my full height, which is six feet tall. My only chance for survival was to be a class clown, so that's what I became for the next four years. My expectations for myself were so low. I think I kept them low on purpose because there was no way I could compete with people who seemed to have it all together. I was a very late bloomer. Oddly enough, most women I know today were late bloomers. We're still sort of trying to get it together! Now I think it's just fine to be a late bloomer. I think it's important for all of us, especially women, to be patient with ourselves.

There will always be those girls that hit it big by fifth grade and end up being the ruling queens by the tenth grade, but the question to ask is, Where do they go from there? There is so much pressure in schools: pressure to be ready for middle school, so you can be ready for upper school, so you can be ready for college. I think people need to take the time to develop themselves as only they can.

• • • • • •

COKIE ROBERTS
Broadcast journalist, author

born: 1943

WHO SHE IS:

Cokie Roberts is chief congressional analyst covering politics, Congress, and public policy for both ABC News and her weekly television show, *This Week with Sam Donaldson and Cokie Roberts.* She is also a news analyst for National Public Radio and author of *We Are Our Mothers' Daughters,* a book highlighted by personal anecdotes that addresses significant issues facing women today.

Tastes in music may have changed, but not much else has since Cokie Roberts was in school, trying out new experiences and getting involved. She loved going to an all-girls' high school and chose to attend the all-women Wellesley College. She took her studies seriously and believes that lessons about the importance of friendship—finding friends to trust and form lifelong bonds with—were as important as any course she ever took.

৯৬

My sister and I went to Stone Ridge, a private Catholic girls' school run by the rigorously intellectual but also deeply fun-loving Religious Sisters of the Sacred Heart. The nuns took us seriously as young women, making it clear that we could be anything we wanted to be in this society. (I tease them now that the only role they tacitly closed off to us was that of priest, and they clearly weren't happy about that.) We were part of the group of kids who ran the student government, acted in plays, organized the events, put out the school newspaper and yearbook. I was the klutzy one, but the others all starred on the athletic teams, which even in that era counted at a girls' school. The daring stuff we did was so square as to be embarrassing—sneaking cigarettes, driving by boyfriends' houses to see if they were home, listening to Johnny Mathis and the Kingston Trio when we should be studying. Little did we know then that the friendships formed from those silly pastimes, the countless hours on the telephone, the sleepovers where no one slept, would in later years bring us back together through happy times and sad—through marriages, and births and deaths, runaway kids and runaway husbands.

• • • • • •

MARGARET MEAD
Anthropologist
1901–1978

WHO SHE IS:

Margaret Mead was an anthropologist known for her groundbreaking understanding of adolescent girls. Her first book, *Coming of Age in Samoa,* studied Samoan adolescent girls in relation to American adolescent girls. Her findings concluded that culture, not genetics, primarily influences personality development.

Even though education was serious business in Margaret Mead's family, she was uncomfortable with her father's double standard—he preferred her to attend nursing school rather than college. Determined to pursue her goals, Margaret went to DePauw University and moved on to Barnard College, where she became interested in anthropology. Though her family moved often when she was a child, Margaret always carried a heavy academic load, made the costumes for school plays, and even kept house for her family.

❧

In school, I always felt that I was special and different, set apart in a way that could not be attributed to any gift I had, but only to my background—to the education given me by my grandmother and to the explicit academic interests of my parents. I felt that I had to work hard to become part of the life around me. But at the same time, I searched for a greater intensity than the world around me offered and speculated about a career. At different times I wanted to become a lawyer, a nun, a writer, or a minister's wife with six children. Looking to my grandmother and my mother for role models, I expected to be both a professional woman and a wife and mother.

• • • • • •

JUDY BLUME
Writer
born: 1938

WHO SHE IS:

Judy Blume is the author of over twenty meaningful and funny books about the struggles and surprises of adolescent life. Titles such as *Are You There God? It's Me, Margaret, Superfudge, Blubber,*

Just as Long as We're Together, and *Forever* have won her more than ninety awards. Ms. Blume's readers send her over a thousand letters a month, sharing their feelings and concerns. She has also written three novels for adults.

Judy Blume came of age in the fifties—a time of soda fountains, bobby socks, and Patti Page, the singing rage. Before she was twelve Judy believed everything was possible; yet by adolescence she felt her dreams weren't realistic. Now Judy understands that regardless of which era adolescent girls grow up in, they all experience these feelings. The pressure to fit in at school often takes precedence over individual satisfaction.

❧

When I look back and think about the child I was versus the adolescent I became, the younger me was a much more interesting person. I had such an active imagination. I never knew boredom growing up, which doesn't mean that I didn't enjoy hanging out with my friends, but I was fine by myself, too. As I grew older it became much more important to hang out with friends all the time. Of course, this was my choice and it was all pretty healthy. It's just that my inner self took a back-seat after the age of twelve.

From the beginning my father always led me to

believe that I could do anything. And this is how I thought of myself until I was twelve. When I became a teenager, my fantasies began to change. I dreamed of love and romance instead of what I might do in the world. I became a conforming adolescent, just like all my friends, striving for popularity. Our lives revolved around boys. Still, as long as I was at school, I truly enjoyed my creative outlets. I was an editor of the newspaper, I danced, I sang, I performed in plays. I was enthusiastic and had passion, but it wasn't focused on anything in particular.

I also want to stress how important it is to READ READ READ! All my life, I've been inventing characters in my mind. It wasn't until later in life that I connected my passion for reading to my passion for writing. By simply reading and being inspired by books written by others, I've found the strength and encouragement to go on, even when I thought I couldn't write another word.

● ● ● ● ● ●

ZORA **Writer** NEALE HURSTON 1891–1960

WHO SHE IS:

Known for her novels and anthropological folklore, Zora Neale Hurston was a member of the Harlem

Renaissance, a cultural movement of the 1920s and 1930s that marked the first time mainstream publishers and critics took notice of African-American literature and arts. Ms. Hurston's best-known works are *Their Eyes Were Watching God* and her autobiography, *Dust Tracks on a Road*.

The death of her mother jolted Zora Neale Hurston's world. She was only nine years old, in Eatonville, Florida, when her mother died and she was sent to live in Jacksonville with her brothers and sisters. In her new town blackness stood out. Whites and blacks didn't mix as freely as they did in her hometown. Zora never felt like she fit in. In school her classmates considered Zora a nuisance. She missed her mother so much that at times she imagined her away on a trip and not dead at all.

&

In the classroom, I got along splendidly. The only difficulty was that I was sassy. I just had to talk back at established authority and that established authority hated back talk worse than barbed-wire pie. In addition to receiving a licking or two for my sassy mouth, my brother was asked to speak to me. But on the whole, things went along all right. My immediate teachers were enthusiastic about me. It was the guardian of study-hour and prayer meetings who felt that their burden was extra hard to bear.

School in Jacksonville was one of those twilight things. It was not dark, but it lacked the bold sunlight that I craved. I worshipped two of my teachers and loved gingersnaps with cheese and sour pickles. But I was deprived of the loving pine, the lakes, the wild violets in the woods and the animals I used to know. No more holding down first base on the team with my brothers and their friends. Just a jagged hole where my home used to be.

At times, the girls of the school were lined up two and two and taken for a walk. On one of these occasions, I had an experience that set my heart to fluttering. I saw a woman sitting on a porch who looked at a distance like Mama. Maybe it was Mama! Maybe she was not dead at all. They had made some mistake. Mama had gone off to Jacksonville and they thought she was dead. The woman was sitting in a rocking chair just like Mama always did. It must be Mama! But before I came abreast of the porch in my rigid place in line, the woman got up and went inside. I wanted to stop and go in. But I didn't even breathe my hope to anyone. I made up my mind to run away someday and find the house and let Mama know where I was. But before I did, the hope that the woman really was my mother passed. I accepted my bereavement.

• • • • • •

BODY
AND SOUL

❧

Nurture Yourself Inside and Out

Everything about you and around you is changing: your friends, your relationship with your parents, and definitely your body. You are likely to question more and listen less to your parents. That's okay. Welcome to this very confusing stage of your life. Complicated choices or difficult decisions are not impossible to handle when you're equipped with the right attitude.

Do the Right Thing. It makes sense and sounds easy, but peer pressure is one of the biggest tempters during this time. Trying to fit in and do what others want you to do is exhausting and frustrating, and often results in hurt feelings and misguided advice. Take it from the women who have been there. They are in a position to reflect and offer examples of what works and what doesn't. They can't solve your problems or take away your pain, but they can guide you by sharing their stories. So whether you are plagued by peer pressure, adjusting to your monthly period, or just feeling left out, let the words spoken by these women help you to know you are not alone.

Listen to the voice inside you. Be good to yourself. Worry less about what others think. Trust yourself to do the right thing when you look in the mirror each morning, and reflect on the day when you lie in bed each night. Learn from those crummy days and savor the joyful ones when everything goes just right.

It's about nurturing yourself, inside and out. Appreciate and take care of your body. Lean on women you respect to help guide you through the process. Listen to music, explore nature with a friend, read often, write in a journal, love your pets—these are the actions that comfort your soul and feed your brain with positive energy. And with patience and time you'll eventually figure out the comfort zone that works best for you. So take a bath and soak in all your glory. Celebrate and nurture the new you!

❧

Friendship with oneself is all-important, because without it one cannot be friends with anyone else in the world.

Eleanor Roosevelt

FANNIE FLAGG
Writer
born: 1944

WHO SHE IS:

Fannie Flagg is the author of three novels, *Daisy Fay and the Miracle Man,* her best-seller, *Fried Green Tomatoes at the Whistle Stop Cafe,* which she later adapted for the screen, and *Welcome to the World, Baby Girl.* Known for her southern style and clever wit, Ms. Flagg also cohosted and wrote for the television series *Candid Camera.*

From age six the southerner Fannie Flagg wanted to write but suffered from dyslexia, though she didn't know it at the time. What she did know was that she couldn't spell, which made learning difficult. Throughout her school years Fannie struggled, coping the best she could. During her career in television she kept her learning disability a secret. That changed when she won an award at a writers' conference. The boost helped Fannie take her desire to write seriously. It was then that she sought help for her dyslexia. She's been writing best-selling novels ever since. Fannie remembers peer pressure being the number-one lethal weapon when she was girl. Steer clear, she says, and do your own thing.

✌

Peer pressure. Of all the dangers during this time of life, the greatest for a young girl is peer pressure. It can literally steal your individuality away from you. I have seen this happen so often. Some teens want so desperately to feel accepted and popular, they will do anything to fit in, to be just like others. What many girls don't understand is that fitting in may not be the right thing to do. It certainly wasn't for me. Looking back, I am so glad I did not fit in, even though at the time I was pained by it. I knew I did not want what the other girls wanted. The peer pressure exerted on my generation of young women was to get married, have children, and stay home. I always wanted to have a career and make my own way in the world. There were times I wished I could have been like all the others. I often felt lonely and out of step with the world—certainly the world of my other schoolmates.

But today, if I could go back to my childhood and change anything it would be this: instead of feeling bad about not being like everybody else, not fitting in, not following the crowd, I would go back to that girl I used to be and say, "It's all right, you are you and the best is yet to come." But of course I cannot go back. I can only warn other girls about the fear of feeling that you are different or that you do not think like all your other friends. I encourage young girls to keep this fact in mind: your peers are also struggling to fit in, to be like they think others want them to be. The girl that does everything like everyone else may very well have no idea who she is and what she thinks or feels about anything. Lots of girls follow the crowd. Many have ruined their lives by believing being popular meant everything. The girls who will do anything to fit in—smoke, drink, have sex early— are misguided. It's not cool to fit in at any price.

Don't fall into that trap. Examine everything you do by really asking yourself *why* you are doing it. Don't like certain music or ways of dressing or behaving just because you feel pressured by friends. Use your head. Don't become one of the sheep, mindlessly following the crowd. Be yourself. Like what *you* like. Believe what you believe. And if you do this now, I can pretty much guarantee that when you go back to your high school reunion in ten or twenty years, you will be surprised to see that those girls you weren't like now want to be just like you!

• • • • • •

ALISON TOWNSEND
Poet, essayist

born: 1953

WHO SHE IS:

The writer Alison Townsend teaches English, creative writing, and women's studies at the University of Wisconsin, Whitewater. She writes poetry and creative nonfiction and has been published in numerous literary magazines, such as *Prairie Schooner, The Georgia Review, Kalliope,* and *The Southern Review.* Her poem "Supplies" appeared in the poetry book *Boomer Girls.*

A lison Townsend was fourteen when she wrote her first poem. She hasn't stopped and embraces poetry as a spiritual discipline. Finding the words to describe an experience as exactly as possible is the goal for Alison, because doing so helps her better understand the world she inhabits. Alison also believes that writing has the power to heal. She was often troubled by the conflicted relationship she had with her stepmother. In her poem "Supplies" Alison first describes her pain and then discovers a gift given to her by her stepmother.

&c

SUPPLIES

Because I believed my stepmother hated me,
because I'd sat alone in the school auditorium
the day all the sixth grade mothers came
and watched a film called Growing Up and Liking It
with their girls, I didn't tell her anything
when it arrived for the first time,
but went straight from the bus to my room

and sat with my legs clenched
around the institutional-sized Kotex
the school nurse had safety-pinned
to my stained Carter's panties.
"I assume you have supplies?" she'd said,
yanking up the panties so hard it hurt.
I didn't, but lied, knowing it wasn't
a question by the way she avoided my eyes,
hoping I'd find an answer in the dog-eared
booklet with anatomical drawings,
pictures of pretty girls
with perfectly combed hair
going swimming or riding,
and cheery captions urging me to
"Remember, you can do all things you usually do!"

I had no supplies.
No quilted pink box like the one
my friend Caroline showed me,
tucked in a drawer with her mother's brassieres,
the little pads stacked, neat and white
as piles of linen, tampons in crackling paper,
("for when I'm older," she whispered,
touching them with a reverent hand)
and the stretchy, lace-trimmed belts
in different colors like ads I had seen
in Tiger Beat *for Frederick's of Hollywood.*

I'd done my reading, but I wasn't prepared.
And so sat in my room, aching, while the bright
arterial red turned a deep rust that smelled
strange and smoky, alive and dead
at the same time, praying it would end.
But it kept flowing, no matter what I did,
until I went to her, desperation
winning out over fear.

And though our years together
are mostly about what didn't work,
I cannot forget the plain white belt
she took from her dresser and slid
around my hips, adjusting a clean napkin
until it fit me exactly right,
and how she kissed me then, hard
in the middle of the forehead,
and explained how to soak
blood stains out in cold water.

● ● ● ● ● ●

TYRA BANKS

Fashion model, actress

born: 1973

WHO SHE IS:

Tyra Banks's image has adorned the cover of
nearly every major fashion magazine and Victoria's

Secret catalog. Ms. Banks founded TZone, a summer camp to encourage independence and high self-esteem among young females. She has also appeared in several movies.

Today Tyra Banks makes her living on her looks, yet when she was a young girl that dream didn't seem remotely possible. Always the tallest kid in the class and extremely thin, Tyra felt awkward and uncomfortable—not the spirit of a future supermodel. She finally grew out of that gawky stage but remembers how her body changes affected her whole attitude. Well aware that beauty is not only skin deep, Tyra polishes the business side of her life as well. She actively raises money and awareness for worthwhile organizations, especially those that benefit children.

৯৶

If there's one period in my life that I don't ever wish to relive, it's puberty. The awkward stage started when I was eleven years old. Over about a three-month time span, I lost nearly twenty pounds and grew three inches. Of course, the growth spurt made me tower over everyone in my class, including the teacher! I was five feet nine inches tall, as thin as a rail, and miserable. I was so skinny that even my teachers began to worry. They all thought I had an eating disorder. My mother took me to the best doctors to try and find out if I had a medical problem, but after poking me with needles and monitoring me on machines, they unanimously agreed that I was in perfect health and that there was absolutely nothing to worry about. They all said that one day I would just start gaining weight.

But of course that was easier said than done. Before my body went through all these bizarre physical changes, I was extroverted, had a lot of friends, and was always in trouble for trying to show off and be the class clown. But when I lost the weight and grew so tall, I became self-conscious and introverted. I rarely showed my face in public, and when I did, it was buried in a book. . . .

As I moved into my teens and all the popular girls at my school started to develop breasts and hips, my body just stayed the same—straight and narrow. I don't think I felt good about my figure until I turned seventeen, when I began to gain weight.

● ● ● ● ● ●

JUDY BLUME
Writer

born: 1938

WHO SHE IS:

Judy Blume is the author of over twenty meaningful and funny books about the struggles and surprises of adolescent life. Titles such as *Are You There God? It's Me, Margaret, Superfudge, Blubber, Just as Long as We're Together,* and *Forever* have won her more than ninety awards. Ms. Blume's readers send her over a thousand letters a month, sharing their feelings and concerns. She has also written three novels for adults.

In childhood Judy Blume often lived in her creative inner world. She enjoyed playing by herself and credits her lively imagination with leading her into writing. Judy grew up in Elizabeth, New Jersey, and attended an all-girls' public high school. She's proudly loyal to her friends, still maintaining childhood friendships that began fifty years ago. Today, Judy Blume remembers herself as a happy and active teenager, yet she also has regrets about not being true to herself.

৯৯

I enjoyed my friends, but hid my feelings from them. In those day we all did, just as my mother hid her true feelings from me. I pretended to be the child I thought my parents wanted me to be—a child who always felt fine about everything even when I didn't. My perception of my mother's expectations was that I shouldn't ever have problems. She wanted me to be happy all the time. Of course, that's not possible, so I went underground with my feelings, never admitting that anything was wrong. I wish I had been more courageous. I wish I had spoken out more often.

I was small and thin at a time when thin wasn't in. The fifties ideal was womanly—full-breasted, rounded hips—Marilyn Monroe, not Kate Moss. In sixth grade I longed to be like my friends, who were sprouting breasts and had started their periods. One day I tried taping cotton balls to my chest, but since I had no bra I must have looked very odd. In seventh grade, when I finally got a bra, I made the mistake of stuffing it with toilet paper, until one night at a school dance, a boy I really liked said, "What's in your bra . . . toilet paper?" And that was the end of that.

I was obsessed by the idea of puberty for a year, like Margaret in *Are You There God? It's Me, Margaret.* And like Nancy Wheeler, another character in that book, I lied to my friends, telling them that I, too, had started my period. When they didn't believe me, I proved it, by letting them feel the pad I was wearing, the pad I had sneaked from my mother's supplies and stuck inside my underpants. Lying about my period made me feel guilty and ashamed, but I could see no way out without admitting what I had done. So I went on pretending to my friends that my period had begun. I didn't tell my mother my secret. She hadn't started to menstruate until she was sixteen, and I knew that I would probably be a late starter too. I finally got my first period a few months after my fourteenth birthday. I was relieved.

But my breasts remained small. When my daughter and son were in high school they gave me a T-shirt that said, "Flat Is Beautiful." I laughed over that shirt and wore it proudly. I know now, breast size doesn't mean anything! It has nothing to do with how sexy you feel or look.

I urge girls today to think for themselves. Don't be afraid to make a decision that is different from your friends. Don't be afraid to make a mistake, because we all make mistakes and it's okay. From our mistakes we learn, we grow. It's okay to admit it was a mistake, too. Being able to admit the truth, at least to yourself, feels really good.

● ● ● ● ● ●

QUEEN LATIFAH

Musician, actor, author, television talk-show host

born: 1970

WHO SHE IS:

The first female rap artist, whose socially conscious lyrics have won her national attention. Queen Latifah runs her own company, has acted in several television series and movies, and hosts her own daily talk show, *Latifah.* She wrote *Ladies First: Revelations of a Strong Woman,* an empowering story about her journey.

*Q*ueen Latifah takes pride in her body and what it is *capable of—in high school, in Newark, New Jersey, she played on two state championship basketball teams. The Queen doesn't look to Hollywood for role models, knowing very few women can look like the waiflike actresses seen on the screen. Queen Latifah experienced a growth spurt early on, which transformed her little-girl body into that of a woman almost overnight. She remembers her first bra experience because it was not pleasant.*

༄

"Dana, are you wearing a bra?" Miss Tamara asked me. Her question was so direct that I froze in my tracks. I said "No," but I was thinking something like "Hell, no." A bra? I didn't even own a bra.

"Well, you need one," Miss Tamara said.

I was eleven years old, and I had two very unwelcome visitors coming on like gangbusters.

At first, I didn't even notice. I was outside playing kickball in front of our house on Littleton Avenue in Newark, running around like a wild woman with the kids from around my way. Just like always. As Miss Tamara was walking down the street from work, she must have noticed me bouncing around. That's when she pulled me aside to tell me I needed a training bra.

Miss Tamara was this fly lady who had a lot of style, much like my mother. And she was big on the neighborhood girls carrying themselves like ladies.

When I got into the house, my mother noticed me jiggling, too. The next day we went bra shopping. I got a cute, little white training bra but the training wheels were off in no time. Before the year was out, I was barely squeezing my new buddies into a 36C. And I was hearing about it.

It's bad enough going through puberty, but to do it in front of the entire neighborhood is mortifying. It's disheartening that the first signs of womanhood—getting your period for the first time, developing breasts—often make a woman feel embarrassed, self-conscious, confused, and inadequate. I know that Miss Tamara meant well and that she just wanted all us neighborhood girls to be tight, but I would have preferred to discover that I needed a bra on my own. My development—like my sexuality—was something I wanted to keep private. Unfortunately, few women have the opportunity to discover themselves on their own. We wind up being uncomfortable with our bodies, because someone is always pointing out the flaws.

● ● ● ● ● ●

KATHARINE GRAHAM

Newspaper executive

1917–2001

WHO SHE IS:

Katharine Graham was chairman of the executive committee and publisher of the *Washington Post,* the family newspaper she took over after her husband's suicide. Considered one of the most powerful women in America, Ms. Graham played a pivotal role in breaking two major news stories: publication of the Pentagon Papers, which revealed the United States' involvement in the Vietnam War, and publication of the Watergate investigation, which became one of the greatest political scandals in American history. At age eighty Ms. Graham won a Pulitzer Prize for her autobiography, *Personal History.*

*K*atharine Graham has characterized herself as a girl who did as she was told. She came from a family where the axiom "Children should be seen but not heard" prevailed. Katharine remembers her mother as a woman who "saw things as she wanted them to be." As a result, many of Katharine's complaints went unheard. For the most part her nurturing was left to her governess.

❧

My mother didn't much believe in doctors—I hardly ever saw one through most of my youth—and Powelly [Katharine's governess] was a devout Christian Scientist, so illness wasn't acknowledged by her. If we said we had a tummy ache or a cold, she would say, "Just know it's going to be all right"—and off we'd go with any disease or even a fever. I did stay home from school briefly with the mumps and was permitted to lie down on the couch for half a day. Another medical problem was a sprained finger the size of a good cigar from a basketball bouncing off the end of it. My mother sent for her masseuse. The lovely Swedish lady took one look and suggested a doctor, who put it in a splint. My freshman year in high school, I had a loud, racking cough the entire winter. This was overlooked at home, but much discussed in a deafened school as I barked my way through the year. Finally, toward spring, my mother decided that a weekend away in Atlantic City would be beneficial, so she dispatched me with the governess, Mademoiselle Otth, to a hotel on the boardwalk for a cure. A cold rain fell the entire time, and we ran out of money. Only thirty years later, when I was diagnosed with tuberculosis, was it observed by the doctors that the scars on my lungs indicated I had had a previous attack. Whatever it was, I got over it.

● ● ● ● ●

ELLEN GOODMAN

Newspaper columnist, author

born: 1941

WHO SHE IS:

Ellen Goodman adds her personal insight to her biweekly newspaper column about current events, which is nationally syndicated in over four hundred newspapers. Ms. Goodman is also associate editor of the *Boston Globe* and won a Pulitzer Prize for distinguished commentary in 1980.

Ellen Goodman wrote a book with her best friend, Patricia O'Brien, called I Know Just What You Mean. *Some research for the book focused on school years and the impact of negative experiences. Ellen was surprised to find how well some girls handle the issue of cliques but saddened to learn cliques are as prominent now as when she was in school. Her solution to the ongoing battle: be open-minded about differences. There's room for everyone.*

⤜❦⤛

I worry about the influence and power of cliques. They are not a part of a normal, natural "girls will be girls" life. Cliques are to girls what bullies are to boys. In all stages of your life, you will be closer to some people than to others, but the exclusion games that go on in cliques are extremely hurtful to girls. Each friend brings something different to the table. You might like to play sports with one and shop with another. From each friend, we get different things. I encourage girls to discover their true self by not putting too much importance on what others have to say about what's "in" and what's "out." It's really hard, but not impossible.

● ● ● ● ● ●

KIM NG
Professional baseball executive
born: 1968

WHO SHE IS:

Kim Ng is vice president and assistant general manager of the New York Yankees. As one of only a few high-ranking females in professional baseball, Ms. Ng oversees day-to-day operations and negotiates contracts for the players. She previously worked for the Chicago White Sox, where she began as an intern after graduating from the University of Chicago.

Competition has always been a part of Kim Ng's soul. Whether she is in the classroom, on the softball field or the tennis court, or talking to the media, Kim keeps

*her cool by adding a sense of humor. She welcomes
laughter as a refreshing way to grasp perspective on a
situation. Kim also says having the right attitude can
work wonders when you want to do your best. Don't let
negative thoughts slip into your psyche. For Kim, it helps
to take one day at a time.*

෨

A lot of people have asked me how I have accomplished so much at such a young age. That's hard to
answer, but there are several things that have helped
me get through certain situations. The first thing is
what my old softball coach used to call PMA. PMA is
Positive Mental Attitude. This has helped me so much.

When I was a kid, at lunchtime, we would pick
teams for softball. Two captains would choose; one by
one each kid was taken. When I first started playing, I
was always the last one picked. They looked at me—I
was puny—and probably thought, I'm not taking her,
what's she gonna be able to do? I got tired of always
being picked last, so I practiced and practiced. My dad
played catch with me, we'd play running bases, and
pretty soon I wasn't the last kid picked anymore. Eventually, I was the first girl picked, and then I was picked
before some of the boys, and then I was playing in the
New Jersey State Finals as the starting shortstop, and

then I had college coaches asking me to play for them, and then I was coaching and teaching kids how to play. It could have been really easy to say, "I stink, I can't play, I'm the worst one," but instead of seeing failure, I chose to see improvement. I used PMA. Set small goals for yourself, and when you reach one, go for the next one. Whatever you're battling, take one problem at a time.

The second thing that's important to me is laughter. I love to laugh. Even as a kid, I was always trying to get people to smile or to think something was funny. Laughter has always helped me, even as an adult. When I get flustered, I don't say much, instead I try to find the humor, because humor breaks down barriers. It makes people feel comfortable with you. They can identify and relate. It's funny how people let down their guard.

I recently walked into my mom's house, and on the refrigerator was my high school yearbook picture. My younger sisters had made a copy and put it up there. The quote I selected for the yearbook was something like "Always have a sense of humor. Life is too important to be taken seriously." I felt that then and it's still true. We're here and we have all these important jobs, but we have to have fun along the way.

• • • • • •

SHERYL SWOOPES

Olympic Gold Medalist, forward for the Women's National Basketball Association Houston Comets

born: 1971

WHO SHE IS:

Sheryl Swoopes, an Olympic Gold Medalist, is the leading scorer for the WNBA Houston Comets and often voted Most Valuable Player. The Comets have won three WNBA championships under her leadership. Sheryl is also the first female athlete to have a Nike basketball shoe—Air Swoopes—named after her.

Sheryl Swoopes listened to the voice inside her soul. She made it to the big time, though the journey wasn't easy. She and her two brothers came from a single-parent home, unable to afford any luxuries, even an extra pair of shoes, but lack of money didn't stop Sheryl from pursuing her dream. She loved playing basketball, so that's what she did. Each time she got knocked down, Sheryl picked herself up, stronger than before.

෴

Life is going to be tough. You're going to get knocked down, but you have to keep getting back up. The harder you get knocked down, the harder you get

up. Nothing is going to be given to you. The most important thing is to believe in yourself once you set your
mind on doing something. Once you set goals, don't let
anybody—mom, dad, brothers, sisters, friends, anybody—tell you that you can't do it. Remember, if you
don't believe in yourself, nobody else will either. That
always helps me overcome obstacles. No one but me
walks in my shoes, lives my life, knows what I want or
what I can do. Only I know. I believe in myself and have
worked hard to achieve my goals.

● ● ● ● ● ●

ANNE FRANK
Writer, Holocaust victim
1929–1945

WHO SHE IS:

Anne Frank became famous after the publication
of her remarkable journal, *The Diary of Anne Frank.*
The book chronicles the dreams and frustrations of
this young girl hiding from the German Nazis.

*Anne Frank knew about suffering firsthand. Her diary
reveals her most secret thoughts about love, family,
and dreams. Anne never finished growing up because
her life ended in a German concentration camp during*

World War II. Yet while Anne hid from the Nazis, she wrote about hope and what calmed her fears—nature.

♍

The best remedy for those who are frightened, lonely or unhappy is to go outside, somewhere they can be alone, alone with the sky, nature and God. For then and only then can you feel that everything is as it should be and that God wants people to be happy amid nature's beauty and simplicity. As long as this exists, and that should be forever, I know that there will be solace for every sorrow, whatever the circumstances. I firmly believe that nature can bring comfort to all who suffer.

● ● ● ● ● ●

BRITNEY SPEARS
Singer, dancer
born: 1981

WHO SHE IS:

After two attempts the superstar Britney Spears became a member of the Disney Channel's Mickey Mouse Club at age eleven. By the time she was seventeen, Ms. Spears was a household name, topping the music charts with her number-one album, . . . *Baby One More Time.* Her second album, *Oops! . . . I Did It Again,* sold over 1.3 million copies in its first week out. The Britney Spears

Foundation, created with the Giving Back Fund, started a performing arts summer camp for underprivileged kids in New England.

One thing was evident when Britney Spears was a little girl—she loved to perform. She sang constantly and performed wherever she could, especially in the bathroom because she loved the way it sounded. Her mother witnessed Britney's talent and determination and guided her. This optimistic mother-daughter team experienced rejection together, but they never lost faith. Turning rejection into opportunity was what they did best.

છે

I don't think for one minute that my family or I ever had a set plan about how my life would turn out. If there had been an outline to follow—we'll do this, then we'll do that, let's follow A, B, C, then D—I know for sure I would have failed or else been miserable. We just rolled with it, tried new things, took chances, and most of all had a great time along the way. I'm a firm believer that everything is in God's hands and you don't always know what's around the corner. If you knew exactly what lay ahead, what kind of an adventure would it be? If life were so predictable, wouldn't it be boring?

My lessons led to talent competitions, and that led to auditions, and eventually we wound up in New York.

Our philosophy was really "Hey, why not?" I never felt any pressure. It was all about having fun and seeing where fate would take us.

There were so many times when things just didn't work out the way we had hoped (I didn't get on *The Mickey Mouse Club*) and times when we got some nice surprises (I did get on *The Mickey Mouse Club*!). We lost some, we won some. That's just the way it went in the basketball games I used to play in junior high school (I hated when we got our butts kicked, but it happens) and that's the way it goes in life, too. . . .

It's important to stick up for what you believe in, even if others challenge you. I think when you begin to doubt yourself, it's like self-sabotage. As long as you're being true to your goals and working real hard, you have to have faith that everything will fall into place. And if it doesn't right away, you still have to keep on going. You can cry over something you can't control, you can sit there moping, feeling sorry for yourself, or you can just pick youself up and try again. I did my share of crying, but it never lasted very long. Mama's optimism is contagious, and I guess my hopes were stronger than my fears.

● ● ● ● ● ●

WENDY WASSERSTEIN

Playwright

born: 1950

WHO SHE IS:

Wendy Wasserstein is the author of numerous Broadway plays, including *The Sisters Rosensweig* and *The Heidi Chronicles,* which earned her both a Tony Award and a Pulitzer Prize. Determined to give high school students more exposure to the arts, Ms. Wasserstein created her own theater program, which brings students to seven Broadway plays throughout the year. They keep journals on the experiences and earn academic credit.

For Wendy Wasserstein, the theater is home. Always a believer in the power of the play, she works hard creating intimacy onstage by developing characters audiences can relate to. Maybe it's her street smarts cultivated while growing up in Manhattan, where she attended an all-girls' school, or her gift for listening and being able to learn from others' experiences, or maybe some combination of the two—whatever her magic, Wendy Wasserstein writes stories we love. Her wish for young girls is that they find a home, the place that feels good.

I think adolescent girls have a much more difficult time now than when I was growing up, simply because they are constantly bombarded by unrealistic images of girls they can never be. I find it interesting that during post-liberation, there is far more emphasis on looks, fashion, and weight. I would find it much harder now, and I found it extremely hard then.

When you're young it's very difficult to figure out who you are and even harder to figure out how to go about being who you are. My suggestion is to find out what you like to do. Then do it. This makes a huge difference in life—the extra bonus is you'll meet people with similar interests and it all begins to click. I am putting on a play right now, and though I used to be the youngest person, now I am the oldest person, but it doesn't matter. I am working with theater people. I know these people. I like them and I've liked them my whole life. It works for me and I belong there. To figure out where you belong is a pretty good thing. Don't be with people you think you should like but be with people you sincerely do like. So often in high school you think you should be with the people who really scare you, and that's not true. Surround yourself with people you like and you'll find your way.

● ● ● ● ●

NINA TOTENBERG

Broadcast journalist

born: 1944

WHO SHE IS:

Nina Totenberg is the award-winning legal affairs correspondent for National Public Radio and can be heard regularly on *All Things Considered, Morning Edition,* and *Weekend Edition.* She covers the U.S. Supreme Court, making the legal arguments comprehensible. Ms. Totenberg also writes frequently for major newspapers and magazines.

When Nina Totenberg started working in the then male-dominated world of broadcast journalism, she would lean on her women friends (and still does) for support and advice, much as she did in high school, when her dreams of becoming a journalist competed with dreams of finding Prince Charming. Nina recommends finding peace within yourself before making any radical romance decisions.

ॐ

You know the guy that you are just crazy and insane about? If you don't marry him, I promise that you will see him in twenty years and he will be a dud. You will be so grateful that he didn't adore you when you wanted him to. I have had this experience more than once. When dating and falling in love, there is this feeling of great desperation to find the appropriate mate, but my experience really is that the older and more comfortable you get with yourself, the easier it is to find somebody who you will be happy with and vice versa. There is enormous pressure from society, family members, or even yourself to find the perfect person. Don't make yourself crazy. Don't count on other people to make you happy. Once you are comfortable in your own shoes, the rest will follow.

• • • • • •

JANE GOODALL

Primatologist, National Geographic Society explorer in residence

born: 1934

WHO SHE IS:

In 1960 Jane Goodall arrived in Africa's Gombe Forest to study chimpanzees. Her findings have revolutionized our understanding of primate behavior. Her research revealed that chimpanzees have distinct personalities, that they are meat eaters, and that they use blades of grass as tools to pluck termites from a mound. Today the Jane Goodall Institute continues observing chimpanzees, and Dr.

Goodall travels over three hundred days a year, speaking to audiences about her studies, preserving the environment, and spreading her primary message—that we must be respectful of all life and that every single person can make a difference.

Jane Goodall grew up in England and loved riding horses. Her family couldn't afford riding lessons, so to feed her soul Jane spent weekends tending horses at a riding school. She was so good at caring for them that her responsibilities grew until she was trusted to take clients out for rides. She was thrilled when she was invited to go on a foxhunt, something she had always wanted to do. Her reaction to the experience took her by surprise.

ॐ

Most Saturdays I went to a riding school in the country owned by the remarkable Selina Bush, known as Bushel. Vanne [Jane's mother] could not afford to pay for me to ride every week so I used to clean the saddles and bridles, and muck out, and help on the farm. I worked so hard and so enthusiastically that I was often rewarded with a free ride. Most of Bushel's animals were small, hardy New Forest ponies that had been taken, as foals, from the herds that ran wild in the nearby forest. Riding them was how I gradually learned the art of horsemanship. One day, to my enormous delight, I was allowed to ride a show pony. Sometimes I went in for jumping competitions at local gymkhanas. And then I was offered the chance to go hunting. Fox hunting.

How exciting! It meant that I would ride with the huntsmen in their "pink" coats, which in fact are red as red can be. There would be huge hedges and fences to jump; there would be the sound of the hunting horn. Most important, Bushel clearly believed my riding was good enough to meet the challenge. I determined not let her down.

I didn't think about the fox. And then, after three hours of hard riding, I saw him, bedraggled and exhausted, just before the hounds seized and tore him up. In that moment, all the excitement vanished. How could I for even one second have wanted to be part of this murderous and horrible event? Why did I want to horseback ride with grown-ups while others followed in cars and on bicycles to see a great pack of baying dogs chase after one poor little fox? . . .

I have wondered a lot about that hunt. The very fact that I, an animal lover, had wanted to take part seems extraordinary now. What if I hadn't seen the fox at all? Would I have wanted to go again? What if we had lived in the country and had horses of our own and I had been expected to go hunting from an early age? Would I have grown up accepting that this was the thing to do?

Would I have hunted foxes again and again, and watched dispassionately as they suffered, "all pity choke by custom of fell deed"? Is this how it happens? Do we do what our friends do in order to be one of the group, to be accepted? Of course there are always some strong-minded individuals who have the courage of their convictions, who stand out against the group's accepted norms of behavior. But it is probably the case that inappropriate or morally wrong behaviors are more often changed by the influence of outsiders, looking with different eyes, from different backgrounds. Fortunately, I was not put to the test. None of my family's friends were of the hunting set; I could drop out of the picture without causing even a lifted eyebrow. But I continued to love riding horses, and I did, to my shame, go hunting one more time many years later in Kenya.

● ● ● ● ● ●

JACKIE JOYNER-KERSEE

Track and field Olympic and world record champion

born: 1962

WHO SHE IS:

Jackie Joyner-Kersee is an Olympic champion who has become the fastest, and the longest- and highest-jumping female athlete in track and field to date.

Nobody does it better than Jackie Joyner-Kersee. That's because Jackie never gave up. At her community youth center she loved participating in every sport. Basketball was her first love, even though track and field made her famous. There were bumps along the road, but Jackie's coaches guided her through the maze often poisoned with racism and sexism. Jackie believed she had the talent and courage to be a star. For Jackie, a little hope went a long way.

❧

Never give up on yourself and never let your dreams die. If you just have a little glimmer of hope, when everyone else doesn't believe in you anymore, don't give up. If you believe it can happen—then you have the power to make it happen. Always be respectful of yourself. Love yourself, and it will be easier to respect others and love others. Everything is a learning process.

● ● ● ● ● ●

CYBILL SHEPHERD

Actress, model, singer

born: 1950

WHO SHE IS:

Cybill Shepherd's successful modeling and acting career began in the 1970s. She launched her acting career with her starring performance in *The Last Pic-ture Show.* Her two hit TV series, *Moonlighting* and *Cybill,* won many awards and entertained millions. Her autobiography is called *Cybill Disobedience.* Cybill also enjoys singing and performs across the country.

In the 1970s Cybill Shepherd's porcelain face and silky blond hair adorned the covers of Vogue, Glamour, *and* Life *magazines. While growing up in Memphis, Cybill didn't give her beauty much thought. She preferred play-ing outdoors and participating in school to primping. As her body began to change, no one told her that soon she would start menstruating. When she did, the experience came as quite a shock.*

᪥

I hadn't a clue why there was blood on my under-pants at camp the summer I was eleven—Mother had skipped that subject altogether. I imagined it as a stig-mata, a penance for willful tomboyishness, or perhaps evidence of a rare and incurable gastrointestinal disor-der. I padded myself with toilet paper until one of our teenage counselors discovered I was the source of the cabin's T.P. shortage and provided me with a long over-due biology lesson. When I summoned up the courage to report my new status as a woman to my mother, she shook her head in commiseration, muttering something about "the curse." In the school bathroom, I would stand frozen in the stall, working up the courage to walk nonchalantly to the wastebasket with my wrapped-up sanitary napkin. I cannot overestimate the significance of the invention of flushable tampons.

Before menstruation, I was physical and athletic and strong. I could run, jump, climb higher than any boy. I earned Shark Club membership at camp (for swimming the most laps) and wrestled with the lifeguards at the pool in unbridled horseplay. Suddenly, I had no choice but to act like a lady, which seemed like a dangerous narrowing of perspectives.

• • • • • •

PHOEBE ENG
Writer, activist

born: 1961

WHO SHE IS:

After practicing law in New York, Hong Kong, and Paris, Phoebe Eng founded *A. Magazine: Inside Asian America,* for the English-speaking, Western-oriented Asian market. She is the author of *Warrior Lessons: An Asian American Woman's Journey into Power* and lectures extensively on empowering women to be true to themselves. An award-winning social activist, Ms. Eng advises many national organizations on race relations. She was a member of the Ms. Foundation delegation to the 1995 UN World Conference on Women in Beijing.

Phoebe Eng strives to be true to herself. Pleasing her parents while pursuing her dreams sometimes created an inner anxiety that confused her. Today Phoebe finds peace when standing at land's end. This solitary experience makes her feel a part of a bigger universe and not so alone. Find a tranquil place for yourself and look up at the stars. You can feel the warmth and support of others who have been down this path.

꙳

When the moon is full, I get into my car and drive to the ocean alone. There, I see people like me, wrapped in blankets or heavy sweaters, who have also been pulled from the comfort of their warm homes toward the vastness of a shore that looks like a lunar surface, with flickers of light that skip like an electric current on the waves.

In the solitary moments of a clear, moonlit night I stand on my own, looking upward toward the sky, and am reminded that I am part of a pattern that is tremendous and timeless. There is comfort in knowing that people have gazed at the night skies as I do since the beginning of time and will continue long after I am gone. And on this full moon night, there will be those who venture to their own coasts, to the beaches of India and Mombasa, Denmark and Thailand, and along the Mediterranean. I go to the beach on these nights to know that I am ultimately connected to everything and everyone around me, forever.

As connected as we are—to friends, to family, to each other—we often feel we are ultimately on our own as we make our way through life, and that can be a frightening prospect. We can overcome this fear by reaching out to one another, and in our shared courage, we will learn.

● ● ● ● ● ●

PASSION
POWER

❧

Make Your Dreams Come True

Your adrenaline is pumping and you're smiling so hard it hurts. Scoring the winning soccer goal leaves you breathless. Riding horses soars you into outer space. And you don't just love to dance, you feel compelled to dance. You've got passion power. It's that intense feeling inside that takes you places you've never been before. The first time you realized your full potential, you were hooked. It felt right—all that mixed up energy inside was finally focused, it had a goal. Welcome its arrival and stick with it, because passion is what makes you feel so alive, what makes dreams come true.

Discovering your own passion is exhilarating and helps you become independent. With an open mind and the right attitude, your passion will emerge. Some people are lucky enough to experience many passions in their lifetimes because they live life to its fullest, always trying new things. Sheryl Swoopes was told she shouldn't play basketball because she was girl. Following her passion and trusting her instincts, Sheryl is now a WNBA championship basketball player. Since childhood, nature was in Sylvia Earle's soul. When she discovered the ocean Sylvia fell passionately in love with its inhabitants. Today she is living her dream as a renowned scientist and leader in the exploration and preservation of our oceans. It all starts with commitment. Both women persevered until their dreams became reality. You can, too.

Who are you? List your dreams. Whatever they are, there are women who can help you make them come true. Take the time to recognize those who support your efforts. Share your ideas and goals with an interested person who has traveled down this path. Follow your passion as these women have done. So, whether it's studying music at Juilliard, writing for *Rolling Stone* magazine, scuba diving around the world, or becoming the first woman president of the United States, you have the passion power to make your dreams come true. *Go for it!*

There are people who put their dreams in a little box and say, "Yes, I've got dreams, of course, I've got dreams." Then they put the box away and bring it out once in a while to look in it, and yep, they're still there. These are great dreams, but they never even get out of the box. It takes an uncommon amount of guts to put your dreams on the line, to hold them up and say, "How good or how bad am I?" That's where the courage comes in.

Erma Bombeck

SIGOURNEY WEAVER
Actor
born: 1949

WHO SHE IS:

Sigourney Weaver, a graduate of the Yale Drama School, launched her screen career with the memorable role of Lt. Ellen Ripley in *Alien* and has since played in every sequel. Her versatile acting shines in films such as *Gorillas in the Mist* (she portrayed the primatologist Dian Fossey), *Ghostbusters*, *The Year of Living Dangerously*, *Dave*, *The Ice Storm*, and *Galaxy Quest*. Ms. Weaver loves the theater and is also recognized for her numerous stage performances. When not acting she works with her production company to introduce new voices from the theater to the film industry.

While she was growing up, Sigourney Weaver always felt compared with her successful parents. Her father created the Today *show and* The Tonight Show, *and her British mother attended the Royal Academy in London, where she was active in repertory theater. After graduating from Stanford University with a major in English, Sigourney listened to her heart and decided to try acting as a career. Discouraged at first by graduate school faculty members, Sigourney persevered and followed her passion.*

I can't impress upon you enough what a terrible loser I was for so long. I never would have dreamed of being an actress. When I was in third grade I played the Cheshire Cat and got lots of laughs. And then I got some more decent roles, but when I went away to school, I didn't get cast in leads—I'd only get cast in character parts or male parts because of my height. I went on to college and majored in English with the intention of becoming a teacher or writer, but I kept doing theater on the side. The theater department in the college never interested me. Finally, when I was almost ready to graduate, I went into my adviser's office and said, "You know, these English courses that we've been taking are so dry. Is that what graduate school is going to be like?" And he answered, "Yeah, more of the same."

So I quickly applied and auditioned for different drama schools not thinking I'd get in, but if I did I'd take it as a sign. Then I did get into a couple of schools. I ended up at Yale. They were nice at first until one day they actually told me I had no talent and that I'd never get anywhere. In spite of that negative feedback, my desire to be an actor kept emerging. It was subliminal on purpose, because my heart would have broken had I said too loudly, "I want to be an actor," and then not succeeded. I knew students who used to say, "I want to be the biggest star in the world." I never knew what that meant and always wondered why some people were so willing to expose themselves so much.

It wasn't until I left drama school and moved to New York that I decided to be an actor. I was there with many good friends, including Wendy Wasserstein, who was a budding playwright at the time. Slowly, I came around to thinking I'd be an actor. It took me a while to set the goal, because I was really sure I would never be able to do it. I was very intimidated by the success of my parents. It just seemed that, compared to them, I wasn't good material. I'm still not quite sure why I've been this successful, but I do think being an English major helped me choose good scripts.

Because of the discouragement I received in school, I worked hard needing to prove myself. Looking back, I credit my friends, some from other cultures, who taught me to slow down and just enjoy what was going on around me. I realized that worrying about things I had no control over was a waste of time. We are all eternal students, learning from each other and the experiences we've had. Besides good health and a good education, the joy of being able to find something you can make a contribution to is the greatest gift. The idea that you can make a small difference will direct you enormously.

● ● ● ● ● ●

BABE
Olympic track and field champion, professional golfer
DIDRIKSON ZAHARIAS
1914–1956

WHO SHE IS:

With Hall of Fame careers in both track and field and golf, Babe Didrikson Zaharias was America's greatest female athlete from 1932 (her Olympic wins) to her death. Intense and self-confident, Ms. Zaharias excelled in basketball and exhibition baseball before turning her attention to golf. In 1950 she and five other women golfers formed the Ladies Professional Golf Association, the LPGA.

Babe Didrikson Zaharias was a born athlete. Her passion for competitive sports started at an early age and saw her from one victory to the next. Basketball championships in Texas led her to track and field events, where she set Olympic and world records in hurdles, javelin, high jump, broad jump, and baseball throw. In the 1930s there were no opportunities for Babe to earn a living in track and field, so she took up golf. By the 1940s she was considered the best woman golfer in the country. Forming the LPGA secured Babe's financial future and made her famous by showing the world that women athletes could attract fans. Babe's passion paved the way.

❦

Before I was even into my teens, I knew exactly what I wanted to be when I grew up. My goal was to be the greatest athlete that ever lived. I suppose I was born with the urge to get into sports, and the ability to do pretty well at it. And my dad helped to swing me in that direction. He followed the sports news in the papers, and he'd talk to us about it. I began reading the sports pages when I was very young myself; I can remember that even then I was interested in famous golfers. Poppa kept reading about the Olympics in the newspapers, and telling us about the star athletes over there. I got all steamed up. I was fourteen years old at the time. I said, "Next year I'm going to be in the Olympics myself." . . .

I couldn't accept the idea that I wasn't good enough for the basketball team. I didn't think the girls who were on it were anything wonderful. I was determined to show everybody. To improve myself, I went to the coach of the boy's team, Lil Dimmitt. I said to myself, "The men know more about basketball than the women." I'd use my study hours to practice basketball. I'd show the teacher that I had my homework done and get excused from study hall. I'd go to Coach Dimmitt and worry him to death with questions about how to pivot and shoot free throws. He took the time to help because he could see that I was interested. I was a junior before they gave me a chance on the Beaumont High girls' team. We went to different towns to play other high schools and we beat them all. And I was the high scorer from the start.

● ● ● ● ● ●

JACKIE JOYNER-KERSEE

Track and field Olympic and world record champion

born: 1962

WHO SHE IS:

Jackie Joyner-Kersee is an Olympic champion who has become the fastest, and the longest- and highest-jumping female athlete in track and field to date.

After watching a television program about the great athlete Babe Didrikson Zaharias, Jackie Joyner-Kersee was inspired to try her hand at many sports. With an extremely disciplined and rational approach, Jackie succeeded in everything she tried. Her approach was simple: be consistent and do a little better in each race. Babe would have been proud.

❧

A lot of the friends I had were mostly teammates, and it was very difficult for my friends who weren't in sports to understand why I wanted to spend all my time on the track or to practice during the summertime in the heat. They couldn't relate to my ambition. I felt it was what I had to do. It is really the makeup of the individual and her commitment to her goals. Even though others might not understand, it's not their decision. It's up to the individual to set her own standards and live up to them without regrets. I wanted to be good, but the difference was, I didn't want to be good overnight. My motto then was one day at a time. In track, I wanted to improve just a tenth of a second in each race. During my first time running, I came in last. But I knew after each time out, even if I was in eighth place, if I improved a tenth of a second then I was getting better. That's what I wanted to do. I wanted to know that after all the hard work that I put into training, I was getting better each time. I didn't have to come in first all the time, but if I improved my speed, that would mean I'd go faster.

● ● ● ● ● ●

ANNE FRANK
Writer, Holocaust victim

1929–1945

WHO SHE IS:

Anne Frank became famous after the publication of her remarkable journal, *The Diary of Anne Frank.*

The book chronicles the dreams and frustrations of this young girl hiding from the German Nazis.

Anne Frank's enormous talent as a writer is evident in her journal. Her daily devotion to writing reveals her natural ability to express what so many girls her age feel, even today, in countries around the world. In words that have not been edited, Anne writes eloquently about her own dreams and passions. Had Anne Frank survived, her passion for the written word in all likelihood would have deepened until she became the famous writer she so longed to be.

৯৩

I finally realized that I must do my schoolwork to keep from being ignorant, to get on in life, to become a journalist, because that's what I want! I know I can write. A few of my stories are good, my descriptions of the Secret Annex are humorous, much of my diary is vivid and alive, but . . . it remains to be seen whether I have talent. And if I don't have the talent to write books or newspaper articles, I can always write for myself. But I want to achieve more than that. I need to have something besides a husband and children to devote myself to! I want to be useful or bring enjoyment to all people, even those I've never met. I want to go on living even after my death! And that's why I'm so grateful to God for having given me this gift, which I can use to develop myself and to express all that's inside me!

When I write I can shake off all my cares. My sorrow disappears, my spirits are revived! But, and that's a big question, will I ever be able to write something great, will I ever become a journalist or a writer? So onward and upward, with renewed spirits. It'll all work out, because I'm determined to write!

● ● ● ● ● ●

QUEEN LATIFAH

Musician, actor, author, television talk-show host

born: 1970

WHO SHE IS:

The first female rap artist, whose socially conscious lyrics have won her national attention. Queen Latifah runs her own company, has acted in several television series and movies, and hosts her own daily talk show, *Latifah.* She wrote *Ladies First: Revelations of a Strong Woman,* an empowering story about her journey.

Always cheered on by classmates and encouraged by her parents to follow her dreams, Queen Latifah knew where she was headed—music. Her thought-provoking lyrics are aimed at empowering women, not assaulting them, like many rap songs tend to do. Now a successful rapper, the Queen got her start where many entertainers do, on her school's stage.

৯৩

I was scared the first time I went onstage in a talent show at Irvington High School. I couldn't breathe, and I broke out into an instant sweat at the thought of going out in front of all those people. What if they don't like me? What if somebody boos? Those questions are usually enough to get people to hide behind the curtain and never come out onstage. Instead I turned it around. What if they love me? What if they give me a standing ovation? Both my lack of self-confidence and my abundance of it were speaking at the same time. The latter won out.

I loved singing, and I wanted to know if other people would enjoy the music I made as much as I did. I would never know if I really had talent unless I went out there. I took that stage and sang "If Only for One Night" by Luther Vandross. I focused on a smiling face in the crowd. I didn't know the person, but he was encouraging me, and I took it. I got that standing ovation. The next time I stood onstage, I was still scared, but not as much.

There's nothing wrong with being afraid. There is

something wrong—definitely wrong, with being so afraid that you don't even try. I've always been more afraid of not trying something. If you try and fail, at least you know what you can't do, and it leaves you room to attempt something else and keep going for it until you find your niche. But if you never try, that's the biggest failure.

• • • • • •

CYBILL SHEPHERD
Actress, model, singer
born: 1950

WHO SHE IS:

Cybill Shepherd's successful modeling and acting career began in the 1970s. She launched her acting career with her starring performance in *The Last Picture Show*. Her two hit TV series, *Moonlighting* and *Cybill*, won many awards and entertained millions. Her autobiography is called *Cybill Disobedience*. Cybill also enjoys singing and performs across the country.

Cybill Shepherd can't imagine not singing. Whether it's a ballad, a pop tune, or a jazz number from the 1940s, Cybill embraces songs that allow her to express herself. Entertaining came naturally. At a young age

Cybill picked up a ukulele, and the passion to sing and perform has been with her ever since.

❧

Most of my childhood was spent in a one-story brick house on Highland Park Place (you could stand at the front door and see straight through to the backyard) with a fake fireplace mantel, plastic violets in a vase, and a mechanical bird that sang in a cage (a gift from my grandmother). One of the few genuine furnishings was a leather-top table that became a disaster of watermarks from cocktail glasses. My mother pasted S & H green stamps into books and redeemed them at the catalog store on Union Street for a prized lamp with a silk shade. I took a cold bath on nights when my sister's rank as firstborn gave her priority and there wasn't enough hot water to fill the tub a second time. Neither was there money for the piano lessons I wanted, much less the instrument itself. So I borrowed my grandmother's old ukulele and songbook I found in her attic and taught myself everything from "In the Evening by the Moonlight" to "Ja Da." Whenever my parents had guests, they insisted I entertain. When I finished my songs everyone always seemed slightly underwhelmed. This definitely eroded my confidence, but nothing, it seemed, would ever stop me from singing: It was something I just had to do, like walking or breathing.

● ● ● ● ● ●

ELEANOR ROOSEVELT

U.S. First Lady, writer, humanitarian

1884–1962

WHO SHE IS:

Known throughout the world for her devotion to human rights, Eleanor Roosevelt was the first wife of a president to take an active role outside the White House. She fought fearlessly for the rights of the poor, women, children, and African-Americans.

A woman of great integrity, Eleanor Roosevelt knew firsthand what it means to follow your dreams. In spite of extreme shyness Eleanor welcomed the opportunity to make a difference in the world. First as the president's wife and then as a political leader herself, Eleanor took huge risks and was courageous in her journey. Embracing her ambition, she accomplished her goals and then some.

❧

Some people consider ambition a sin, but well-trained it seems to be a great good for it leads one to do, and to be things which, without it, one could never have been. Of course it is easier to have no ambition and just keep on the same way every day and never try to do grand and great things, for it is only those who have ambition and who try to do who meet with difficulties and they alone face the disappointments that come when one does not succeed in what one has meant to do. . . . But those with ambition try again, and try until they at last succeed.

● ● ● ● ● ●

ESMERALDA SANTIAGO

Writer

born: 1948

WHO SHE IS:

Esmeralda Santiago is a renowned writer whose works include two autobiographies, *When I Was Puerto Rican* and *Almost a Woman.* Both explore the difficulties of merging two cultures. She has written one novel, *America's Dream,* and also produces documentary films.

*E*smeralda Santiago *learned English by reading children's picture books at the library and eventually became conversant enough to act as her mother's interpreter at the welfare office. Recognizing Esmeralda's potential, a school guidance counselor helped her gain entrance to the New York High School of the Performing Arts. Relieved to escape a clique of abusive girls, Esmeralda thrived there and, though she was enrolled in the acting division, dance gave her inspiration.*

☙

My junior year at Performing Arts turned out to be my best. My average was excellent, aided by near perfect grades in geometry, which after three attempts, I'd mastered. . . .

I was a hall monitor, charged with checking that students wandering around during classes had a pass signed by a teacher. My favorite hall to monitor was on the dance department floor. I sat where I could watch a ballet class in session, could see the dancers hurl themselves through space, their controlled abandon making my own muscles ache for movement. I was envious of the training that made them so graceful and strong, the intricate steps they performed as the teacher called each movement in French.

The training for actors at Performing Arts was modern dance, its language English, its purpose to keep us from embarrassing ourselves if we had to perform musical theater. But I'd come to love dance class more than acting. While I knew I wasn't a great actress, I could see I was one of the better dancers in the drama department. I practiced all the time. The semester we'd studied jazz and learned isolations, I'd begun to practice minute movements of my torso, hips, and back while waiting for the train, or while sitting in history class. At home I couldn't sit still in front of the television while we watched *Candid Camera* or *The Jackie Gleason Show*. One eye on the screen, I stretched, did splits, counted out hundreds of pliés in first, second, third, fourth, and fifth positions while my sisters and brothers complained that my movements distracted them. To pick up something from the floor, I bent over from the hips, back straight, to stretch my thigh and calf muscles. I used the kitchen counter for a barre, leaped from one room to the other, held my leg up to my cheeks like the can-can dancers on *The Ed Sullivan Show.*

I knew I'd never be a ballerina; that wasn't my intention. At Performing Arts we learned that if actors had to wait ten years to make a living at their art, dancers were lucky if they could get that many years out of theirs. For me, dance was not to be shared but to bring me to a place nothing else did. I danced for myself, even when being led across a shiny floor by a skillful partner. It didn't matter if no one saw me dance. It only mattered that I could.

● ● ● ● ● ●

JANE GOODALL

Primatologist, National Geographic Society explorer in residence

born: 1934

WHO SHE IS:

In 1960 Jane Goodall arrived in Africa's Gombe Forest to study chimpanzees. Her findings have

revolutionized our understanding of primate behavior. Her research revealed that chimpanzees have
distinct personalities, that they are meat eaters, and
that they use blades of grass as tools to pluck termites from a mound. Today the Jane Goodall Institute continues observing chimpanzees, and Dr.
Goodall travels over three hundred days a year,
speaking to audiences about her studies, preserving
the environment, and spreading her primary message—that we must be respectful of all life and that
every single person can make a difference.

*Jane Goodall knew early on it would be difficult study-
ing animal behavior in Africa. Yet her perseverance
took her there to spend years studying chimpanzees in
their natural habitat. Braving the jungle, which included
surviving encounters with leopards and lions, she discovered the intelligent side of chimpanzees we would not
know about had she not lived in their environment. Reading and writing were her other passions. As a child, she
spent much time in a tree reading poetry.*

ॐ

One of the reasons I enjoyed reading the Bible was,
I think, because of the sheer poetic beauty of much of
the prose—much of which is lost in the modernized version. I loved poetry and read a great deal. I had catholic
tastes, but at that time I was especially enamored of the

works of Francis Thompson, Keats, Shakespeare, Milton, Robert Browning, and Alfred Noyes. And the war poets such as Rupert Brooke and Wilfred Owen. I was also in love with the poetry of Walter de la Mare. Because we could never afford new books, I used to spend hours in secondhand bookshops, browsing in the poetry section. I loved the feel of those with soft leather covers, and bought as many as I could find—and afford. I had an entire row of them—my "squidgy poets"—in my room. Many evenings I stayed up late reading these poets—or working on a poem of my own, for one of my dreams then was to become, one day, Poet Laureate of England. The themes of my early poems ranged widely. Some were playful, but many, like "The Duck," combined my love for the natural world with my interest in spiritual topics.

꒰꒱

THE DUCK

A duck that flew across the sun
Flew on past me,
Winging his solitary way
Towards the sea.

I saw the brightness of his eye
So close he flew;
His feathers in the sunset gleamed
With lustrous hue.

I heard the music of his wings,
The song of flight
Stirring the stillness of a world
Awaiting night.

I sensed the warm life in his breast
So close to me
And in my heart the pain of joy
That such could be.

The lovely dunes; the setting sun;
The duck—and I;
One Spirit, moving timelessly
Beneath the sky.

Clearly, at that time, I was starting to feel myself a part of a great unifying power of some kind. Certain things caused feelings of such profound happiness that tears would come to my eyes—"and in my heart the pain of joy that such could be." I never knew when such emotions would be triggered: an especially beautiful sunset; standing under the trees when the sun suddenly burst from behind a cloud and a bird sang; sitting in the absolute hush of some ancient cathedral. At moments such as those, I felt strongly that I was within some great spiritual power—God.

● ● ● ● ● ●

Olympic Gold Medalist, forward for the Women's National Basketball Association Houston Comets

SHERYL SWOOPES   born: 1971

WHO SHE IS:

Sheryl Swoopes, an Olympic Gold Medalist, is the leading scorer for the WNBA Houston Comets and often voted Most Valuable Player. The Comets have won three WNBA championships under her leadership. Sheryl is also the first female athlete to have a Nike basketball shoe—Air Swoopes—named after her.

*S*heryl Swoopes is grateful for the opportunities professional basketball has given her—the chance to travel, try new things, meet new friends and, most important, become a role model for all young girls who have the same dream she did. The commitment and competition combo is the name of the game for Sheryl. In junior high, while she was having fun on the court, a coach noticed Sheryl Swoopes's passion.

ॐ

I eventually played Little Dribblers, where I finally found other girls that were also interested in playing basketball. But it wasn't until the eighth grade that the varsity high school basketball coach came down to watch us practice. I felt pretty good because I felt like he was watching me. I thought this was my opportunity to go out and have a good practice and show him what I could do, but he didn't say anything after practice so I thought that was it.

It was not until my freshman year that I started seeing the change in my basketball friends who'd played with me in junior high. A few of them still played, but most switched to cheerleading. I wasn't interested in doing that, and I couldn't have afforded it anyway. So a couple of them still played basketball, but the difference was that they were on the freshman team and I was moved up to varsity. At that point, it seemed that we were going different directions. That's when things really started changing. I started to change my priorities and became even more committed. For a freshman to play varsity meant a lot, and I was very excited about it.

It doesn't take a lot for me to motivate and do something, because once I set my mind to it, I want to be my best. I give it one hundred percent. Even now I don't have a trainer. I have done it on my own for so long that I know what I have to do. It doesn't shock me that I made it. It's overwhelming to me, and there isn't a day that goes by when I don't wake up and thank God for everything He's done for me, but I do stop and say,

"Wow, I did it. I made it and never gave up." My two brothers and I grew up in a single parent home. It was very hard, and we didn't have a lot. I had one pair of tennis shoes that I wore to school and played basketball in, because we couldn't afford another pair.

People get so excited about getting the opportunity to meet celebrities and movie stars. That's great, and I love being able to call myself a role model, but I want all girls out there to know that I'm just a normal, average, everyday person. I've worked so hard to get here, and because of everything that I've accomplished people look at me as a celebrity, but I don't. My message is that anyone can do it.

● ● ● ● ● ●

FRIDA KAHLO

Painter

1907–1954

WHO SHE IS:

The legendary Mexican artist, Frida Kahlo painted vivid self-portraits. Her topics include depictions of herself suffering as a result from a childhood accident, her turbulent marriage to her fellow artist the muralist Diego Rivera, and her commitment to the Mexican Revolution. As seen in most of her paintings, Ms. Kahlo dressed in colorful

Mexican costumes, elaborately braiding her hair with flowers and ribbons to identify herself with her country's heritage.

*P*ainting came to Frida Kahlo indirectly. At age fifteen she broke her spine and shattered her leg in a bus accident. Confined to bed for months, she was in chronic pain for the rest of her life. During her recuperation she turned to painting. The trauma she endured became a main topic in her work.

❧

I was bored as hell in bed with a plaster cast, so I decided to do something. For many years, my father had a box of oil colors and paintbrushes and a palette tucked in a corner of his little photography workshop. Purely for pleasure he would go to paint at the river in Coyoacán, landscapes and figures. Ever since I was a little girl, as the saying goes, I had been casting an eye in the direction of the box of colors. I could not explain why. Being so long in bed I took advantage of the occasion and I asked my father for it. Like a little boy whose toy is taken away from him, he "lent" it to me. My mother asked a carpenter to make an easel, if that's what you would call a special apparatus that could be attached to my bed where I lay, because the plaster cast did not allow me to sit up. In this way I began to paint. I never painted dreams. I painted my own reality.

• • • • • •

MARIAN ANDERSON
Opera singer
1897–1993

WHO SHE IS:

Marian Anderson is one of the great opera singers. She also played a pivotal role in our civil rights history. In 1939 Howard University asked Ms. Anderson to perform at Constitution Hall in Washington, D.C., but the Daughters of the American Revolution (DAR), owners of the hall, denied the request because of Marian Anderson's skin color. In protest, First Lady Eleanor Roosevelt resigned her DAR membership and arranged for Ms. Anderson to perform a concert at the Lincoln Memorial. Ms. Anderson was also the first African-American to sing for the New York Metropolitan Opera.

Marian Anderson early on became accustomed to appearing before an audience. From the time she was six, the church was her stage, the place where she soared and sang as freely as she liked. She loved how singing made her feel and knew she had talent. In her teens the church decided to do something for "their Marian" and took up a collection. In desperate need of a new dress for her performances, Marian was able to buy material to make a new outfit. She and her family were grateful for the support, and her new dress made Marian very proud.

෨

As I moved into my teens, singing at the church took on more importance. When I was thirteen I was invited to join the adult choir. I accepted gladly, and I continued my work with the junior choir. In fact, I sang with both groups until I was past twenty.

Singing was a serious business with me, and I had a deep sense of responsibility about my work with the choirs. Our church was large. The senior choir sang in the upper balcony at one end, and our minister was at the other end. Without knowing anything about the tricks of the trade, I sang naturally, free as a bird, with a voice of considerable size and wide range. There was no difficulty in filling the church auditorium. In my youthful exuberance I let myself go, and on several occasions it was suggested gently that my voice was a little too prominent.

I had no thought about technique or style. It may seem boastful to say so, but at that moment I did not need them. I had no difficulty with any music set before me, for I could sing any note in any of the registers. Usually I sang the alto part, but I could fill in for the soprano or tenor. If necessary, I also filled in for the baritone or bass, though in that case I would sing an octave higher. When the choir sang an anthem, if one of the soloists was absent I was given the nod. The minister would always recognize my voice and make some comment about it. That was my reward.

I became convinced that my presence in the senior and junior choirs was not only a duty but a necessity for the church and me, and I never missed a Sunday. The congregation made me feel that I was an indispensable part of what went on there. It was a stimulating experience.

● ● ● ● ● ●

MARY Actress
TYLER MOORE born: 1936

WHO SHE IS:

The television and film actress Mary Tyler Moore has been America's favorite TV sweetheart since she was first seen in the 1960s playing the perky newlywed Laura Petrie on *The Dick Van Dyke Show* and then, in the 1970s, the clean-cut, single career woman Mary Richards on *The Mary Tyler*

Moore Show. She has appeared in many films, won an Oscar nomination for her role in *Ordinary People*, and was honored with a Special Tony Award for her Broadway performance in *Whose Life Is It Anyway?* Ms. Moore is also the international chairman for the Juvenile Diabetes Foundation. She has lived with diabetes for much of her life.

*B*y the age of seven Mary Tyler Moore had mastered her living-room stage act of singing and dancing for her aunt Bertie and Grandma, with whom she lived most of the time. She proudly modeled herself after Hollywood legends such as Arlene Dahl. When they moved near the Ward Sisters Studio of Dance Arts, Mary's dream of dancing lessons became a reality. Even though money was tight, Aunt Bertie made it happen. Auditioning for Agnes and Ann Ward proved stressful, but it got Mary in the door, and it fed her soul.

&

Agnes asked if I'd like to show her what I could do. Without a choreographic comma, I burst into a dance that was part twirling, some leaping, sometimes, impossibly, both at once, and many quick little baby steps all followed by a lunge forward, arms outstretched, and a verbal "ta-da."

My heart was thudding with expectation and fear. Everything depended on this woman's verdict. Agnes told me that I obviously didn't know anything about dancing, but, because I seemed to want it so much, she would be happy to have me as a student. As I flew out of the front office, suspending myself in mid-air long enough for it to register, I noted the autographed photo of Arlene Dahl. With a combination of awe and jealously, I vowed that my picture would be on that wall someday, too.

And so I began my lessons, two a week, and also began to feel that at last I had something that made me special. And my schoolwork began to improve proportionately to my mastery of the pirouette. I no longer felt lonely, either. As I learned the dance steps and began to excel, in tap especially, the girls at school started paying attention to me.

● ● ● ● ● ●

MARY Singer-songwriter
CHAPIN CARPENTER born: 1958

WHO SHE IS:

The guitarist and singer Mary Chapin Carpenter has a crossover appeal that reaches a universal audience. Her songs, a combination of rock, blues, country, and folk, capture the struggles and dreams of day-to-day life. Among her awards are five Grammys, two best female vocalist awards from the Country Music Association, and best female vocalist from the Academy of Country Music.

All sports were important to Mary Chapin Carpenter, but her first love was competitive figure skating. However, by the time she reached fifteen she realized she couldn't go much further in the sport. Mary recognized it was time to move on and considers that decision a healthy turning point in her life. She is grateful for the discipline skating gave her, and she's now just as passionate about her music. Mary vividly remembers the tough times of adolescence. Finding something special to do helps tremendously.

❧

I wish I could spare someone the pain of growing up. But to help, I remind girls to realize that the feelings they experience are universal. It's so hard to remember that you are not the only one going through this. I would first tell girls not to succumb to peer pressure. It's so difficult not to when you want to be a part of the group, but you must be true to yourself along the way. I encourage every young girl to find her passion. Because being passionate about something is like someone handing you a true gift, a ticket to live. To be inhabited by your passion is a wonderful feeling. To feel not only inspired but moved enough to take action. This is how you accomplish things, make progress and grow. I truly believe passion affects the world in a positive way.

When one learns to be constructive and passionate about something, she can think things through better and understand sooner that everything around her does affect her. Everyone can have a role as soon as she decides she wants one. Just because you may not be old enough to vote doesn't mean you can't learn something and be effective in the process. Pay attention and be involved.

● ● ● ● ● ●

SYLVIA
EARLE

Marine biologist, ocean preservationist, National Geographic Society explorer in residence

born: 1935

WHO SHE IS:

Sylvia Earle is a renowned scientist. She was leader of the first female team of aquanauts, she holds the world record for the deepest solo dive, and she is a protector of oceans. Dr. Earle has spent over six thousand hours submerged in the water. She has solved many underwater mysteries and discovered new species.

By the time she was twelve, Sylvia Earle's curiosity to know everything about the ocean was already intense. Once she became a marine biologist Sylvia lived her dream and accomplished many firsts: she was the first to live with an all-female crew in an underwater laboratory, the first to dive deeper than any person had gone, descending 1,250 feet in a diving suit strapped to the front of a small submarine. Once she landed on the ocean's floor, the strap was released and Sylvia was free to explore. Her journey into the deep is one to celebrate. Sylvia encourages girls to stick with their passion.

৯৫

If you want to be the first to go where no one has ever been before, you can. If you want to discover new kinds of animals, new plants, and whole new systems of life, they are there, deep in the sea. You can be the first to explore any of thousands of undersea mountains and cross unknown plains; be the first to figure out how barely known creatures live, how they spend their days and nights, how their lives influence us—and how we who live on land affect them. I know such things are possible because I have had the fun of doing them and have glimpsed at how much more there is to discover.

Don't let people discourage you from following your passion and your dreams. Over the years many people have told me how they regretted letting go of their dreams, how they wished they hadn't listened to those who said they couldn't make a living doing what they loved to do. If you have found something that makes your heart beat fast, then don't let anyone talk you out of it. Even if it seems like you can't make a living, if you love it, you'll find a way. People with passion are the ones who become the best at what they do. They find ways to make it work. What's tragic is that so many people are talked into doing something they don't love and aren't necessarily good at.

We're so blessed to live in a country that offers freedom and in a time that offers so many choices. Some people are afraid, even terrified, of making choices. They'd rather be told what to do. Can you imagine living in a country that dictated what path you must follow? Can you imagine following a path that is entirely inappropriate for your talents or interests? Americans are so blessed to live in a country that offers the opportunity to be whatever you want to be. You can make the greatest difference. Just keep going. You can find a way.

● ● ● ● ● ●

PERMISSIONS

Interviews were conducted with the following women:
Judy Blume
Mary Chapin Carpenter
Sylvia Earle
Ellen Goodman
Jackie Joyner-Kersee
Kim Ng
Patricia Polacco
Sheryl Swoopes
Nina Totenberg
Wendy Wasserstein
Sigourney Weaver

INDEX

KATHARINE GRAHAM   GLORIA STEINEM

                        MAYA ANGELO

    MARGARET MEAD

                   NINA TOTENGERG

ELEANOR ROOSEVELT

                        MARY TYLE

JANE GOODALL   IRE

                QUEEN LATIFAH

    SIGOURNEY WEAVER   SHERYL SWOOPES

CYBILL SHEPHERD

                        ELLEN GOOD

ZORA NEALE HURSTON

                        FANNIE FLAGG

                   MARIAN ANDER

    CAROL BURNETT

    BEVERLY CLEARY

                   DORIS KEARNS G

MARGARET BOURKE-WHITE

                        CANDICE

    ESMERALDA SANTIAGO